Trust, Legality and Exceptionalism

Trust, Legality and Exceptionalism

Baocheng Liu

Christoph Stückelberger

Einar Tangen

Globethics.net China Ethics Series No. 11

Globethics.net China Ethics Series

Director: Prof. Dr Obiora Ike, Executive Director of Globethics.net in Geneva and Professor of Ethics at the Godfrey Okoye University Enugu/Nigeria

Series Editors: Prof. Dr Liu Baocheng, Founder and Director of Center for International Business Ethics (CIBE) at University of International Business and Economics in Beijing/China. Prof. Dr. Dr. h.c. Christoph Stückelberger, President and Founder of Globethics.net, President of Geneva Agape Foundation GAF, Visiting Professor of Ethics in Beijing/China, Enugu/Nigeria, Moscow/Russia, Leeds/UK.

Additional Volume Editor: Einar Tangen J.D., Economic and Political Affairs Commentator at CCTV, CGTN, CRI, China.org.cn, Xinhua, Al Jazeera, Press TV, TRT World, CNN News 18, etc. Founder and Chairman of China Cities Bluebook Consulting and Principal of DGI/SMP DESIGN.

Globethics.net China Ethics Series 11
Baocheng Liu, Christoph Stückelberger and Einar Tangen, *Trust, Legality and Exceptionalism*
Geneva: Globethics.net 2022
ISBN 978-2-88931-464-5 (online version)
ISBN 978-2-88931-465-2 (print version)
© 2022 Globethics.net

Managing Editor: Ignace Haaz

Globethics.net International Secretariat
150 route de Ferney
1211 Geneva 2, Switzerland
Website: *www.globethics.net/publications*
Email: *publications@globethics.net*

All web links in this text have been verified as of October 2022.

TABLE OF CONTENTS

FOREWORD

Trust is uniquely human. In a world of unprecedented interdependence, this notion is brought to the apex with regard to quality livelihood across cultures because no single social actor – individual, company or nation – can survive on their own in complete isolation. In the old days, trust can be expressed with a simple handshake. Nowadays as our life is intertwined in complexity, we can acquire more certainty relying on the rule of law. If trust is considered a virtue, legality provides the bottom-line for those who are willing to engage. Nonetheless, a good law, from legislation, adjudication and enforcement, should be always there to uphold just principles. Perversion of which shall lead to illegitimacy and provoke rebellion or retaliation. Laws in the international arena is cemented on the fundamental respect to each sovereign nation; there no power above a sovereign. Therefore, exterritorial jurisdiction must be exercised with great caution and within defined limits. Hegemony in the name of law is nothing more than a game of bully.

The current and growing competition between USA and China as two superpowers reduces trust. It is linked to efforts of superiority, especially visible in the sectors of technology, military, trade, research, education and international standard setting and - especially in the U.S. - substantiated with the claim of exceptionalism.

This book looks at the concepts, cases and expression of exceptionalism in the current geopolitical context, in the USA and in different countries, which see themselves as exceptional with an exceptional mission. The first article also looks at ways to build trust by Environmental, Social and Governance standards (ESG). The authors represent perspectives from US, Europe and China as well as different disciplines such as law, economics, political science and ethics.

The United States of America has thrived on the land of promise, charged with a mission for life, liberty and the pursuit of happiness. But it neither justifies its notion of exceptionalism when most of other nations are advancing along the same path with varied forms though, nor warrants its legitimacy intervening the domestic affairs of other nations on equal footing.

Exceptionalism is the claim of a nation to have a unique mission and vocation in the world. After the collapse of the Soviet Union in 1991, the concept exceptionalism resurged among a number of U.S. elites inasmuch as it turns out to be the sole remaining global superpower. Other large and small nations also claimed it throughout history. China as a nation with the nostalgia of its long historical glory punctuated by its century of humiliation is laden with a burning desire to thrive and is no longer ready to condescend to external gesticulations.

The establishment of formal diplomatic relations between USA and China coincided with China's reform and open-door policy at the end of 1978. Over around four decades, China's economic miracle had taken the world with a surprise. It was the U.S. strategic intention that by supporting China to the global community China could turn into a full democracy consummate with U.S. definition which U.S. goods, capital and technology could find a mammoth market. Nonetheless, this goal is only half achieved. Chinese economy has flourished to the point that more than 120 of its companies are seated among the Fortune 500 list and its billionaires have outnumbered the U.S. peers. China's unique norm of governance is further entrenched. Private companies such as Alibaba and Huawei are beating U.S. competitions. Bilateral relationship has witnessed deterioration since the Trump administration on the accusation that China has taken unfair advantage and thereby a strategic adversary. As a result, in addition to blockage of key technologies, a slews of measures have been deployed to deter the rapid global expansion of Chinese firms. The way how Huawei is victimized is an outstanding example.

No one can unwind history, but the history depicted by Francis Fukuyama has not ended. The world is not getting flat either as described by Thomas Friedman. However much divergence the world is experiencing at the current juncture, it would be impossible for these two biggest superpowers to decouple in totality. It is high time to ring the alarm for political and business leaders to revisit those basic ethical principles and values, which are common and can serve humanity on the path of human dignity, economic prosperity with equality and environmental survival. These ethical principles and values are linked to observing legal diligence in order to regain the trust necessary for manageable cooperation as well as fair competition.

Liu Baocheng
Christoph Stückelberger
Einar Tangen

Beijing/Geneva, September 2022

1

CORPORATE ESG IN TRUST-BUILDING THE CASE OF HUAWEI

Shuxiao Liuand, Baocheng Liu

Abstract: Trust is undoubtedly the single most important bond that sustains the shared community of our humankind.[1] When business permeates every corner of society, the trustworthiness of corporate value and behavior exerts an unprecedented impact on our livelihood. This article attempts to examine the essential role of Corporate Social Responsibility ("CSR") in the globalized neighboring-stranger context. A particular focus is to figure out how Environmental, Social, Governance ("ESG") disclosure or non-financial disclosure contributes to fostering corporate trust and trust-building. The pertinent ESG performance of the Chinese giant Huawei in the highly sensitive and competitive information and communication technology industry ("ICT") is critically scrutinized as a case in point.

Key Words: Trust-building, CSR, ESG, Transparency, Huawei

---

[1] Shuxiao Liu is a J.D. candidate at Rutgers Law School – Newark, New Jersey, USA. Baocheng Liu is Director of the Center for International Business Ethics and Associate Dean of the Academy of Innovation and Governance, University of International Business and Economics, Beijing, China. Shuxiao Liu is a J.D. candidate at Rutgers Law School – Newark, New Jersey, USA.

1.1 Trustworthiness: A virtue of societal necessity

Trust is the foundation in human interaction and healthy relationships as it satisfies the basic need for psychological safety among all parties involved who aspire to be their own masters, rendering the entire process and outcome predictable and discernable, and henceforth reliable and accountable. While all religions promote divine trust, the ancient Chinese philosophy in Confucius Analects offers more secular teachings: without trust, a person does not stand, a company does not prosper, a nation declines.[2]

Many beliefs and traditions have disappeared in history, but the lapse of time does not render the notion of trust obsolete. On the contrary, it becomes more crucial in our modern era with the emergence of paradoxical neighboring-stranger relationships; people are neighbors in a shrinking global village, and they are strangers because of accelerating information asymmetry in a world of complexity. With the prevalence of capitalism, it is particularly true when our lives are dominated by businesses who possess upper hand knowledge and overwhelming bargaining. As a rudimental ethical principle, those who stand in vantage points are expected to take a proactive stance in the exemplification of trustworthiness. To minimize such disequilibrium therein, voluntary trust-building turns out to be a significant part of all business leaders managing the company-stakeholder relationship both for the sake of moral responsibility and shaping the corporate competitiveness among their peers.

Amongst numerous scholarly definitions, the one developed by Gambetta and revised by Bromiley and Harris enjoys high popularity: "one's

---

[2] 论语•颜渊》：“去食，自古皆有死，民无信不立”;《论语•为政》：“人而无信，不知其可也。大车无輗，小车无軏，其何以行之哉？” Adapted and Extended meaning from two translated excerpts in the Analects of Confucius.

non-calculative belief in another's honest in negotiations, good-faith efforts to keep commitments, and forbearance from opportunism." (Bromiley & Harris, 2006, p. 125).

Liberal economists believe that an economic system works itself (Plant, 1932, pp. 51-52; Robertson, 1936, p. 83) "being co-ordinated by the price mechanism and society becomes not an organisation but an organism". (Coase, 1937; von Hayek, 1933). They draw a distinction between the provision of public goods and scarcity goods, and therefrom a demarcation line is delineated between the functions of state and market. It is conveniently derived that social equity and economic efficiency would be optimized and presented it a positive feedback loop if the private sector is left to businesses driven by profit while the public sector is totally left to the state for social and environmental welfare using the tax revenue largely contributed by businesses. Nonetheless, this prescription of deconstructivist portmanteau is only an oversimplified hypothesis in that it stands neither the test of market rationality nor the moral conscience of a firm embedded by a dynamic collection of human goals. In the real world, however, this line of distinction is more often blurred by the inevitable externality of a market actor, causing either positive or negative consequences on the society and environment. After all, the market functions to meet the diverse expectations of multiple stakeholders instead of the sole desire of a single group as stockholders. Such a notion can be further deduced to a ridiculous conclusion that an individual can well fulfill his or her responsibility of citizenship so long as he or she earns the wage and pay tax without any social stewardship.

Clearly, Milton Friedman was preoccupied with his grand mission of defending an economic system of free enterprise by insisting that "a corporation is an artificial person" without the legitimacy to bear responsibilities (Friedman, 1970). But his disdainful attitude towards corporate social responsibility by stating that "there is one and only one social responsibility of business - to use its resources and engage in activities designed to increase its profits so long as it stays within the rules of the game, which is to say, engages in open and free competition without deception or fraud" has reaped a windfall of criticism over time (Friedman, 1970). Such proposition rests upon the falsified assumptions that:

a)   a corporation is an economic robot solely programmed for profit seeking instead of an instrument to realize more diverse goals by proprietors/stockholders who are also citizens in the society, including those of social and environmental wellbeing;

b)   the boundaries of business operation is strictly fenced by regulators leaving no dark corners for a corporation to step into.

Besides, a completely legalistic society would entail far larger and more interventionist government, which would run counter to Professor Friedman's own ideals. In the end, Friedman (1970) has to contradict himself or at least compromise with the reality by stating, "That responsibility is to conduct the business in accordance with their desires, which generally will be to make as much money as possible while conforming to their basic rules of the society, both those embodied in law and those embodied in ethical custom." Confucian emphasis on the sense of shame continues to claim validity for every actor, especially for companies engaged in constant competition for profitability, in order to prevent a lawful but shameless game of bottom race.

When the scale of giant firms is akin to a sizeable sovereign state (see Table 1 below), catering to public demands becomes an indispensable part of their economic planning in addition to the needs of the payers. Huawei, an employer of 197,000 people, ranked No.44 with $129,183.5 million revenue that rivals Morocco and Ethiopia with respective GDP of $112,871 million and $107,645 million ranking 59th and 60th in the world (see Table 1 below). Furthermore, to compare with a sovereign state, giant firms are more influential and practical of conscious powers in shaping the value chain over the global landscape serving as hubs that weave the nodes into an integrated business network. As detected by Professor Usher in the thriving industrial age, "it is as the integrating force in a differentiated economy that industrial forms are chiefly significant." (Usher, 1920, p. 10)

Table 1: Corporate Revenue versus National GDP[3]

Rank-ing	Top 10 Companies	Revenues ($M)	Rank-ing	Country	GDP ($M)
1	Walmart	$523,964	24	Belgium	501,795
2	Sinopec Group	$407,009	29	Israel	401,954
3	State Grid	$383,906	30	Argentina	383,067
4	China National Petroleum	$379,130	31	Egypt	363,069
5	Royal Dutch Shell	$352,106	34	Denmark	355,184
6	Saudi Aramco	$329,784	38	Bangladesh	324,239
7	Volkswagen	$282,760	40	Colombia	271,347
8	BP	$282,616	41	Finland	271,234
9	Amazon	$280,522	42	Vietnam	271,158
10	Toyota Motor	$275,288	43	Pakistan	263,687

---

[3] For a more comprehensive view of how Corporates compares to Countries, see and compare *Corporate data based on release for the year 2020 by Fortune.* (2021). Global 500 Fortune Global 500. https://fortune.com/global500/2020/search/ 2022; with Country data based on World Bank. (2021). Gross domestic product 2020 World Development Indicators. https://databank.worldbank.org/data/download/GDP.pdf

Business firms are engaged in the allocation of economic resources via transactions with multiple parties. The cost of transactions resulting from distrust presents a major hindrance not only to market efficiency on a macro level, but also distributive gains on a micro-level. Uncertainty is a major contributing factor to distrust forging a typical prisoner's dilemma described in the game theory. It is placed by Oliver E. Williamson (1981) on the top of the three critical dimensions that may undermine a transaction. Consequently, it prevents the firm from expanding its business and growing out of its parasitic cocoon. R. H. Coase (1937) in The Nature of the Firm brought forth his famous argument over the theory of transaction cost:

> Other things being equal, therefore, a firm will tend to be larger:
> a)   the less the costs of organising and the slower these costs rise with an increase in the transactions organised;
> b)   the less likely the entrepreneur is to make mistakes and the smaller the increase in mistakes with an increase in the transactions organised;
> c)   the greater the lowering (or the less the rise) in the supply price of factors of production to firms of larger size. (Coase, 1937)

"[T]rust not only minimizes transaction costs, but also … has a mutually causal relationship with information sharing, that also creates value in the exchange relationship." (Dyer & Chu, 2003, p. 66). Karl Llewellyn (1931) made a distinction between "hard contracting" and "soft contracting" in business transactions. He observed that "a highly legalistic approach can sometimes get in the way of the parties instead of contributing to their purposes. This is especially true where continuity of the exchange relationship between the parties is highly valued." (Llewellyn, 1931). What he implies here is the mutual trust generated over time between parties that entails the ethical integrity of the parties other than harsh contractual stipulations relying on the strength of legal protection.

Thanks to the wave of market liberalization around the world in the post-Cold War era, barriers obstructing the movement of all production factors are substantially reduced. While more opportunities begin to unfold in "a flat world" – a catchphrase coined by Thomas L. Friedman (2006), businesses are operating in a glass bowl rather than a black box. The paradigm of marketing promotion and competition is under rapid transformation. It is observed that mere investment in sales puffs or promotional window dressing with minimal regard to ethical integrity receives diminishing returns. Under such circumstances, transparency in business leads to trust, which can be considered the starting point to sustainable operation (Kappel, 2019). The benefits are significant, ranging from high employee retention, boosting sales, and ultimately creating reputation and success. In the modern information age, consumers would be more likely to support companies they trust, while deceitful companies will fall off the map (Kappel, 2019). Customers and employees demand stronger communication and transparency, and they likely move on when they don't receive it (Kappel, 2019).

Survey shows that the world is ensnared in a "vicious cycle of distrust", while business is still the most trusted institution (Edelman, 2022). Being viewed as trustworthy, businesses have the responsibility and obligation to be and remain transparent. Trust is not a manageable facial mask; it is a categorical imperative in the discourse of Immanuel Kant, i.e., an indisputable quality endowed with a responsible actor. What one can manage and even financialize, however, is reputation embodied in the corporate image and product brand equity. Modern trends in business management have made it imperative to consider risks beyond classical frameworks and timeframes. As businesses have become increasingly complex, the issue of information symmetry has grown as well. This, in turn, calls for a corporation's self-discipline and regulation. Trust is thus positioned at the focal point of corporate success.

Trust is an interdependent network that influences and binds all actors in an economy. The decline in trust is detrimental to businesses and the economy. As Kenneth Arrow (1972), Nobel Laureate famously states, "Virtually every commercial transaction has within itself an element of trust, certainly any transaction conducted over a period of time. It can be plausibly argued that much of the economic backwardness in the world can be explained by the lack of mutual confidence." Indeed, a business prospers on all its stakeholders' collective trust and confidence.

Social paradigms are apparently cyclic. In the good old days, a close-knitted "villager culture" prevailed. Trust in this communitarianism was generated through a long-term bond when inhabitants know almost everything about each other living together by generations within a limited radius though. Self-discipline is nurtured by social customs and conventions. Misbehavior is deterred by communal denunciation, and disputes are mediated by respectable local seniors. As people became "emancipated" and expanded their realm of activities, they found it necessary to deal with strangers, thus a more distanced "stranger culture" evolved. Under such social context, law, acting in the position of a rational third-party regulator, vested with enforceable authority comes to fill the gap of trust among strangers. With the advancement of technology, particularly in the shipping and information and communications technology ("ICT") industries, coupled with reduced barriers in cross-border mobility, we find ourselves all over a sudden living in a global village, calling for a return of trust-building analogous to the ancient tradition of "villager culture" when law continues to defend the bottom-line of acceptable behaviors. In the narrowest sense, when no businesses would never deny their mission to take care of customers, it is time to go further to take care of what customers care about, now that customers have never before evolved into enlightened citizenry in this globalized society and on this planet Earth.

For businesses, "lasting trust is the strongest insurance against competitive disruption, the antidote to consumer indifference, and the best path to continued growth. Without trust, credibility is lost, and reputation can be threatened." (Edelman, 2021b). While trust is mutual, corporations endowed with economic might and technological advantage are expected to take initiative in order to earn the reciprocal response of multiple stakeholders. Edelman's studies believe that trust is "the ultimate currency in the relationship" with stakeholders, as it defines an organization's "license to operate, lead and succeed", and allows responsible risk-taking and rebounding from mistakes (Edelman, 2021b).

1.2 Disclosure: A starting point for trust-building

The absence of information is a perceptual risk per se since uncertainty avoidance is a natural inclination in everyone's decision-making. Information concealment is disconcerting because people are uncertain of what is up the sleeve of other parties and what is in store for themselves. To be transparent, a corporation would have to disclose information to the public. On top of it, such information has to be unbiased and legible. Recent years have witnessed increasing popularity for Corporate Social Responsibility ("CSR") reporting especially among sizeable firms, but a common issue with it is that corporations act on their own as unilateral storytellers avoiding the involvement of external forces for impartial auditing. Scepticism is thus developed over its truthfulness and faithfulness. Whether a firm's CSR report can be taken seriously in the professional due diligence process is an objective test.

By allowing one's non-financial information to be evaluated by third-party authorities, corporates increase their trustworthiness among their stakeholders. More practically, it saves the cost of information search and due diligence check in business deals. With the growing emphasis on sustainability, good CSR promotes a positive brand image and reputation, while bad performance erodes into corporate brand value. Trust-building goes both inwards and outwards. It is equally important to build trust among the operation and with other external stakeholders.

1.3 CSR: A moral license for business

Among a bewildering range of definitions, the EU Green Paper helped distil its essence of CSR: it "is a concept whereby companies integrate social and environmental concerns in their business operations and in their interaction with their stakeholders on a voluntary basis." (European Commission, 2001, p. 6)

The phrase corporate social responsibility ("CSR") was coined by Bowen (2013) in his seminal book the Social Responsibilities of the Businessman first published in 1953. With the expansion of conglomerate companies, the subject was made popular by R. Edward Freeman (1984) in his celebrated book Strategic Management: A Stakeholder Approach together with the catchphrase "stakeholder", to be followed by an array of key works of Archie Carroll, Peter Drucker, and others. In economics, the tendency of a negative externality is regarded as the basic motivation for businesses to produce more, which results in the imposition of cost onto other parties.

As early as 1971, the Committee for Economic Development ("CED"), a powerful public policy think tank based in Washington D.C., identified in its statement that "social problems might be ameliorated by the efforts of business especially large and professional corporations…businesses should do much more to meet social needs." (CED Research & Policy Committee, 1971, p. 7). In 1991, Professor Donna J. Wood created a framework for assessing the impacts and outcomes of CSR programs, which marked the convergence of CSR from moral advocacy to the quest for measurability (Wood, 1991). Over the past three decades, CSR has become the buzzword for sustainable business practices, partly as a result of accelerated global competition. Through CSR, businesses would benefit society as a whole while enhancing their corporate image and product brands. The more visible and successful a corporation is, the bigger its responsibility is to demonstrate ethical behavior and lead industrywide initiatives.

With the rise of attention to CSR, stakeholder capitalism seeks to further debunk the Friedman Doctrine of "social responsibility" solely to make a profit for the shareholder (Friedman, 1970). At the time of the 1970s, a spearheaded goal on short-term earnings and profits might have been indeed beneficial to corporate governance, whereas modern times have changed with the evolution of corporate mission and game rules for competition. In her book "The Shareholder Value Myth", Lynn Stout (2013) showed that Friedman employed a very narrow definition of shareholder interest, limiting it as strictly financial and wrongfully assuming that all shareholders have identical interests. The birth of CSR also signifies that companies can be both socially responsible and financially profitable, as a firm's stakeholder may value the firm's sustainability efforts, which can result in additional benefits to the firm, including raising corporate morale, promoting brand reputation and trustworthiness, and reduce costs of raising capital (Henisz et al., 2019; Hernández-Murillo & Martinek, 2009). The plain idea is that companies are more likely to succeed and deliver strong returns if they create long-term values for all their stakeholders (Henisz et al., 2019).

Since the turn of the century, three developments are noticeable with regard to the expectation and application of CSR:

a) It is converging from conceptual framework into actionable programs facilitated by more applicable standards and metrics such as the Global Reporting Initiative ("GRI") and Guidance on Social Responsibility ("ISO 26000"), yearning for a method of measurability and outside accountability;

b) It is becoming "voluntarily responsible behavior" of enterprises beyond the realm of legal obligations; more corporations engage in "actions that appear to further some social good, beyond the interests of the firm and that which is required by law." (McWilliams & Siegel, 2001, p. 117).

c) It is becoming a subject of rapid codification raising the bottom-line of corporate behavior. "Certain regulatory measures create an environment more conducive to enterprises voluntarily meeting their social responsibility." (European Commission, 2011, p. 3)

To advance the Millennium Development Goals ("MDGs") followed by the current Sustainable Developments Goals ("SDGs"), the United Nations with the Guiding Principles on Business and Human Rights is pushing the member states in a more specific direction for CSR intervention in the business world through renewed legislation and tightened enforcement. As of now, 15,401 companies across 164 countries have signed up for the UN Global Compact aimed at socially responsible policies and reporting practices in the private sector (UN Global Compact, n.d.).[4]

To illustrate, we will examine how Huawei as leading global information and communications technology ("ICT") solutions giant, whose ICT solutions, products, and services are used in over 170 countries and regions internalize and even economize the SDGs through ESG reporting at the focal point of increased scrutiny. Before that, let us briefly review the history and development of ESGs.

1.4 ESG: A powerful toolkit for trustworthiness

Businesses are increasingly motivated to voluntarily disclose ESG performance as part of their risk management as well as brand enhancement strategies, cognizant of the prowess of reporting system for corporates to walk the talk. They demonstrate the challenge and success of their CSR programs. Healthy governance and transparency are the foundation upon which trust is built and maintained across all stakeholders. In the end, transparency requires extensive communications with stakeholders,

---

[4] See statistics summarized and displayed on https://www.unglobalcompact.org/, accessed on February 14, 2022.

genuine human interactions, and unwavering commitment to trustworthiness.

The concept of Environmental, Social, Governance ("ESG") and Socially Responsible Investing ("SRI") dates back to biblical times, evident in ancient Jewish law (Maimonides, 1470).[5] Modern SRI was initially focused on helping value-based investors to identify ethical issues and "screen out" morally concerning companies ("sin" stocks include tobacco, firearms, or gambling) (Entine, 2003). ESG grew out of SRI, expanding itself as an inclusion criterion rather than an exclusion evaluation of investment options. In 1994, John Elkington (2018) coined the framework TBL, consisting of three Ps, profit, people, and planet. TBL argues that businesses should focus on each of the three Ps and not just on "Profits" since they are equally important for any commercial enterprise to be sustainable. This concept evolved into the focus of ESG (Sridhar, 2021). The term ESG was first officially coined in a United Nations Global Compact 2005 report titled "Who Cares Wins", providing recommendations on how to incorporate ESG issues into corporate management (Knoepfel & Hagart, 2004). Gradually, ESG has become crucial to company risk management strategy (Caldwell, 2021).

Obviously, the concepts of ESG and CSR are highly related under a shared goal. While both are conscious of the social and environmental impact exerted by business activities, subtle differences do exist. The chief mission of CSR is to promote the ideal and generate context about preferable business ethics and corporate policy whereas ESG is focused on the action and measurable outcome. Therefore, CSR is more persuasive with qualitative propositions, whereas ESG drives for quantitative

---

[5] Moses Maimonides. *Maimonides' Eight Levels of Charity*, Mishneh Torah, *Laws of Charity*, 10:7 – 14 (1470) Maimonides, M. (1470). Mishneh Torah, Laws of Gifts to the Poor https://www.sefaria.org/Mishneh_Torah%2C_ Gifts_to_the_Poor.9.17?ven=Gifts_for_the_Poor,_Trans._by_Joseph_B._Meszle r,_Williamsburg,_Virginia,_2003&vhe=Torat_Emet_363&lang=en&with=all&l ang2=en.

measures. The most outstanding distinction lies in the fact that ESG specifically brings to light the dimension of governance within the firm, which is the ultimate determinant of corporate behavior. In other words, it is a meaningful shift from mere outward looking to a bi-directional perspective in terms of corporate responsibility. For this reason, ESG claims higher instrumental function and thereof more often tied in with SRI by investors to gain deeper insight into the mission, vision, value, strategy, and more importantly, the managerial competence of the target company in order to access its worthiness and sustainability.

This is a welcomed development. The world is dominated by businesses, and businesses are increasingly being dominated by capital. Dredger masters tell us that cleaning a river must start at the upper stream. Similarly, a positive chain effect can be magnified when financial institutions begin to take the lead by seriously embracing the concept and practice of CSR as an essential component of corporate trust building. The two rounds of the financial crisis - Asian crisis in 1997 and the global crisis in 2008 - in a matter of a single decade has been calling for a refocus on the responsible policy and behavior of financial institutions. The Public Company Accounting Reform and Investor Protection Act ("Sarbanes-Oxley Act of 2002," 2002) promulgated in 2002, has been known as the severest regulation of the new century in reaction to several major corporate and accounting scandals adding criminal penalties for financial fraudulence. It also requires top management individually to certify the accuracy of financial information. Ironically, after the collapse of Enron, WorldCom, and Tyco International, who were found in violation of the Securities Exchange Act of 1934 by nondisclosure of major financial information and artificially inflating their earnings, Lehman Brothers in 2008 heeded their heels erupting like a volcanic crater spewing toxic lava and gas around the world financial market. This again proves that a legalistic approach has its limitations when people's mind outsmarts their soul.

Here again, Confucius teachings continue to serve as a valuable reminder: "If people are governed legalistically and controlled by criminal penalty, they will cut corners to avoid punishment ignoring the personal sense of shame; if people are governed by virtue and guided by propriety, they will cultivate their sense of shame and thus behave in compliance."[6]

ESG's three central factors are defined and explained by the UN Principles for Responsible Investment ("PRI"), launched in 2006 (PRI, 2018). The six principles for responsible investment are also clearly defined as a voluntary and aspirational set calling for incorporation into investment and ownership decisions revolving around the implementation of ESG issues (PRI, n.d.). [7]

a) We will incorporate ESG issues into investment analysis and decision-making processes;

b) We will be active owners and incorporate ESG issues into our ownership policies and practices;

c) We will seek appropriate disclosure on ESG issues by the entities in which we invest;

d) We will promote acceptance and implementation of the principles within the investment industry;

e) We will work together to enhance our effectiveness in implementing the principles;

f) We will each report on our activities and progress towards implementing the principles.

There are no less than a dozen ESG reporting standards. While all frameworks require reporting on the E, they vary in the focus on S and G

---

[6] 论语》：“道之以政，齐之以刑，民免而无耻；道之以德，齐之以礼，有耻且格。” Adapted from *Analects* of Confucius.

[7] See *The six Principles for Responsible Investment, PRI.* (n.d.). What are the Principles for Responsible Investment? Retrieved February 8 from https://www.unpri.org/about-us/what-are-the-principles-for-responsible-investment

elements. An obvious reason is that environmental impacts are more discernible and measurable. There are five leading frameworks, namely the Global Reporting Initiative ("GRI"), the Climate Disclosure Standards Board ("CDSB"), the Sustainability Accounting Standards Board ("SASB"), the International Integrated Reporting Council ("IIRC"), and CDP (formerly, the "Carbon Disclosure Project"). GRI is designed to be universally suitable for large and small organizations across different types of sectors and industries aiming to inform all stakeholders (GRI, 2021). SASB's primary focus is to assist firms in communicating sustainable information to investors. CDP helps companies reduce greenhouse gas ("GHG") emissions, preserve water resources, and safeguard forests (CDP, 2021). CDSB has no specific metric, but it relies on metrics and KPIs developed by other standards (CDSB, 2022). IIRC focuses on explaining an organization's value creation, preservation, and erosion over time, benefiting all stakeholders (IIRC, 2021).

The emergence of a plethora of standards during the earlier stages of ESG seemed inevitable. Different companies in different regions and industries have different goals and processes, and different stakeholders focus on different things. It would be hilarious to compare a juice factory with an oil company or a normal consumer with an investor. However, too many frameworks and standards often lead to confusion (Murdoch, 2021).

Despite the current approach of "letting a thousand flowers blossom" and giving companies the discretion, recent trends all point to a convergence of ESG reporting frameworks; implicitly allowing companies to freely select the ESG criterion in their own best interest creates loopholes for opportunistic attempts to white or greenwash in the reporting process. This unification of leading reporting frameworks is a good initiative to help stakeholders better identify ESG performance.

Spiked by an overall growing interest of regulators, policymakers, and the accounting profession, the "Big Five" have recently announced a joint statement of intent toward a collaborative and comprehensive reporting framework for ESG disclosure (CDP et al., 2020). "GRI, SASB, CDP and CDSB set the frameworks and standards for sustainability disclosure, including climate-related reporting, along with the Task Force on Climate-Related Financial Disclosures ("TCFD") recommendations." (CDP et al., 2020; Impact Management Project, 2020). "The IIRC provides the integrated reporting framework that connects sustainability disclosure to reporting on financial and other capitals." (CDP et al., 2020; Impact Management Project, 2020).

Not surprisingly, however, under the current circumstances, even with a comprehensive framework, government intervention is still largely absent. This is rallied by the counterargument that we, after all, still prefer to accept the lesser evil - a free-market or Laissez-Faire ("LAISSEZ-FAIRE," 2019), other than a stiff economy under stringent government mandate - where all corporate behaviors are modeled in singular stereotype.

1.5 Huawei with ESG: *exempli gratia*

Corporates need to exhibit a high degree of transparency and disclosure to fulfil ESG reporting requirements. By disclosing its ESG factors, a company displays that it cares not only about profit but also the greater well-being of all its stakeholders. Edelman studies have found that investors merit companies that excel in ESG (Edelman, 2021a). While each ESG program is a unique case for an individual company to incorporate its distinct values and situations, renewed priorities in the expectations of stakeholders must be carefully taken into account. Extensive communication with stakeholders, genuine human interactions, coupled with a dedication to trustworthiness is essential to attain accountability.

To illustrate the importance of ESG in corporate trust building, we examine the efforts and results of Huawei. Huawei's trust-building efforts revolve around three pillars: quality products and services, distinct vision and mission, and impressive ESG performance.

Among 29,389,255 Chinese business entities (China Statistical Yearbook 2021, 2021) whose average life expectancy lasts no more than 4 years (Xin, 2021), why Huawei Technologies Co., Ltd. as a private company in the most competitive ICT industry can stand out not only in size (40th in 2020 by Fortune 500 Global Companies (Fortune, 2021)[8]) but also in globally recognized brand value?

Established in 1987 with a registered capital of 21,000 CNY (equivalent to US$5,645 according to the official exchange rate of the year) in Shenzhen, Guangdong province, Huawei managed to achieve US$99.4 billion revenue in a span of 34 years. What is more impressive is that the company's achievement has been based on organic growth instead of relying on mergers and acquisitions.

The brand value of Huawei registered US$6,196 million in 2021, rated 85th among the Best Global Brands by Interbrands - the only Chinese company on its top-100 list (Interbrand, 2021). Jez Frampton, Interbrand's Chief Executive, said: "HUAWEI's rapid growth and long-term investments in its brand helped it earn a place among the world's most valuable brands. Despite its low brand awareness in the US, HUAWEI has gradually expanded its reach around the world." (Williams, 2014).

Nowadays, brand value stands more for reputation than recognition. While recognition can be bought by heavy investment in promotional gimmicks such as advertising, reputation is earned by trustworthiness. Huawei ranks 8th in BCG's The 50 Most Innovative Companies (BCG, 2021). Apart from its technological prowess in meeting the needs of the market in both quality consumer products and enterprise solutions, ESG performance is a strong impetus for Huawei to earn its global reputation.

---

[8] Most Chinese companies on top of the Fortune 500 are state-owned conglomerates in the banking and energy sectors.

Huawei was among the first batch of Chinese companies that began releasing Sustainability Reports as early as 2008, in accordance with the GRI standards and ISO 26000/SA 8000 guidelines (Huawei, 2020b). It has closely aligned its ESG program according to the 17 UN SDGs in the process of planning and execution (Huawei, 2020b). This 2020 report explains the grand progress that Huawei has made in its four pillars of sustainability and ESGs: "Digital Inclusion", "Security and Trustworthiness", "Environmental Protection", "Healthy and Harmonious Ecosystem". (Huawei, 2020b, pp. 15-16).

The TECH4ALL digital inclusion initiative embodies Huawei's first pillar: leaving no one behind in the digital world (Huawei, 2020b). This project benefited more than 60,000 teachers and students from more than 200 schools, helped 22 protected areas in 18 countries manage natural resources, and protect biodiversity more efficiently (Huawei, 2020b). Additionally, Huawei forged partnerships with more than 1,500 colleges through the Huawei ICT Academy, with close to 57,000 students receiving Huawei certification (Huawei, 2020a). Fifteen accessibility functions to benefit all users had also been added to Huawei smartphones (Huawei, 2020a). Huawei also enabled more than 50 million people in remote areas in more than 60 countries to have mobile Internet access by implementing RuralStar solutions (Huawei, 2020a).

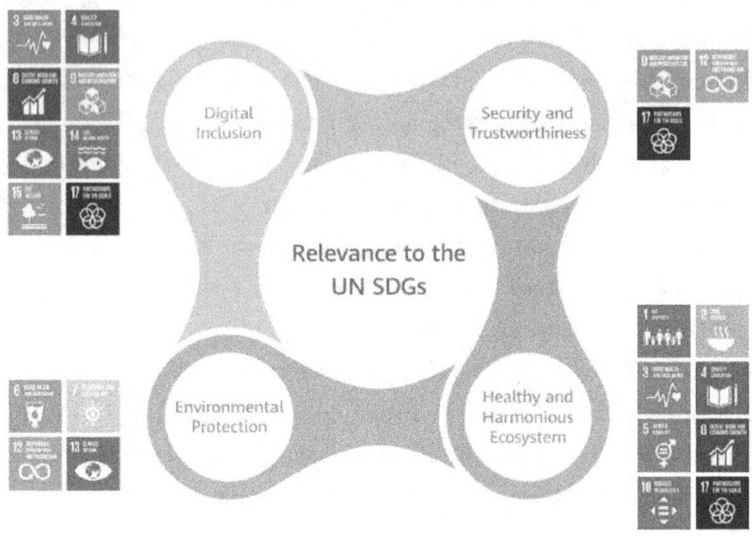

Figure 1: Huawei's 4 Sustainability Strategies and their relevance to the UN SDGs.

Huawei specifically reserved an important pillar for trust building, which is crucial in cyber security and data protection: a) improved "software engineering capabilities and practices, b) built resilient networks, c) developed trustworthy, high-quality products, and d) supported stable network operations and business continuity." (Huawei, 2020b).

In the Environment department, Huawei focuses on three areas: a) "reducing carbon emissions", b) "promoting renewable energy", and c) "contributing to a circular economy" (Huawei, 2020b, p. 59). Based on the popular 3Rs formula - Reduce, Reuse, Recycle, Huawei strives to reduce medium and long-term carbon emissions and encourages its suppliers to follow. It works on green power technology. Its global recycling program has processed more than 4,500 tons of e-waste (Huawei, 2020b). Huawei scored high for its actions to cut emissions, mitigate climate risks, and contribute to a low-carbon economy, among more than 5,800 companies enrolled in the CDP (Huawei, 2020b).

In the Social department, Huawei advocates "Collaborating for the common good" by promoting continuous innovation, community engagement, employee benefit, and philanthropy (Huawei, 2020b, pp. 15-16). In 2020, the company invested 11.89 billion CNY in employee benefits, held more than 100,000 active patents, organized and provided technical assistance to more than 650 charitable activities in nearly 90 countries to respond to the pandemic (Huawei, 2020b).

Huawei's Governance is an interesting and controversial one. Contrary to a widespread western belief, Huawei is an independent, privately held firm from a governance standpoint (Huawei, n.d.). It is neither the rumored state-owned nor militarily controlled enterprise. Huawei is owned by employees through an Employee Stock Ownership Program ("ESOP") that has been in place since the company's conception, and to own a share, one has to work at Huawei (Huawei, n.d.). As of 2018, among the 96,768 shareholding employees, Founder and Chairman Ren Zhengfei only owns a 1.14% stake (Huawei, n.d.). As Huawei claims, employee ownership is the key to their growth (Huawei, n.d.). Huawei's "Employee Shareholding Scheme" ("Scheme") has been questioned by Balding and Clarke in their paper "Who Owns Huawei?" (Balding & Clarke, 2019). They address it as merely "a profit-sharing scheme", therefore postulate that Huawei is not owned by the employees due to its opaque ownership structure, and suspect that because Huawei is owned by its trade union, it is effectively state-owned (Balding & Clarke, 2019). Goto attacks that conclusion, analyzing the origin of the Scheme, the limitation it was designed to overcome, the actual equivalence of "phantom stocks" and regular stocks, the power trinity formed by the phantom stocks, Governance Ordinance", and "Virtual restricted stock management charter", the limitation of the founder's veto rights, the power of the Employee's Representative Commission, all collectively grants ownership rights to the employees, all largely overlooked or misrepresented by the study of Balding and Clarke (Goto, 2021).

In summary, The ESOP creates an incentive for employees to perform, as well as attracts talent.

In light of its current success and influence, Huawei is both a beneficiary and a victim of China's global expansion. As the old Chinese saying goes: a bigger tree crest gathers more wind blows. The collateral effect of the U.S. and China Trade War resulted in Huawei being hit with a series of commercial trade restrictions by the U.S. government. It has been years since the U.S. launched its Anti-Huawei campaign based on security and privacy concerns. Huawei has suffered major blows outside of China, in its software integration and hardware exportation (Whalen, 2021). The U.S. export ban prohibited Huawei phones to carry the Google Play store or other popular Android apps (Moon, 2019). Perhaps the most notable U.S. restriction is the ban of Huawei from using U.S. software and hardware in certain semiconductor processes, forcing it to look for other chip sources (Davis & Ferek, 2020).

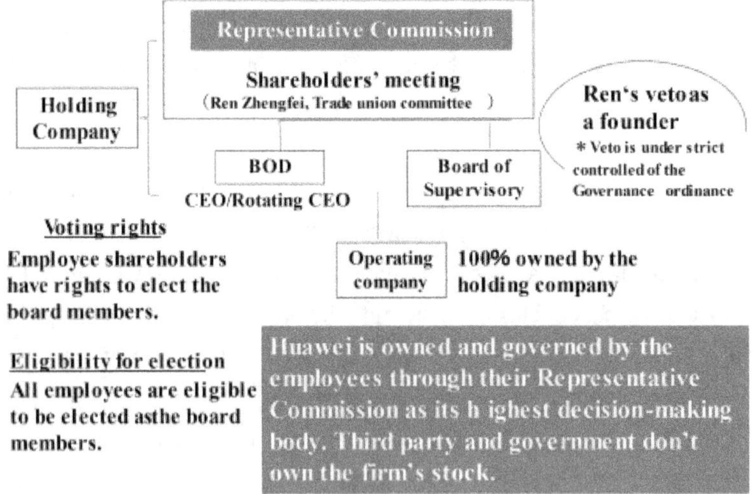

Figure 2: Huawei's Governance Structure.

Although Huawei has denied the allegations that it violated U.S. sanctions on Iran, it's head company, together with its global subsidiaries are nevertheless listed on the U.S. Commerce Department's "entity list" due to national security concerns (Shepardson et al., 2020). The U.S. is not only pulling the plug for key supplies from American companies but also dissuades its allies to rescind deals with Huawei around the globe. However such devastating moves, Huawei is still standing, at least with the support of Chinese nationals (Whalen, 2021).

Huawei is at the center of criticism facing Chinese tech giants, as it participated in the grueling and notorious "996" tech working culture, ultimately deemed illegal by China's Supreme People's Court (Huang, 2021). On top of that, Huawei is well known for its famous "wolf-pack culture", which not only was a stim pack in its rapid development but also was the catalyst of its troubles (Zhong, 2018). Acknowledged by Ren Zhengfei, "many workers did not pay attention to internal rules and controls", perhaps "because Huawei used to evaluate staff sole according to how much business they won." Obviously, there are "red lines" never to step over (Zhong, 2018). However, there are "yellow lines" employees were encouraged to bend, such as "gifting or other inducements", if it can help win the firm benefits (Zhong, 2018). As Huawei expanded globally, these lines seemed to have been blurred. In 2002, Huawei was accused to have broken an embargo, selling technology to Saddam Hussein's regime (Zhong, 2018). Throughout the years, Huawei has been suspected of stealing intellectual property from other competitors (Flynn, 2003; Tabuchi, 2014).[9] Huawei has been accused of bribing foreign officials (Rossi, 2012).

---

[9] In 2003, Cisco Systems sued Huawei for allegedly copying its instruction manual, the case was settled. See Laurie J. Flynn, *TECHNOLOGY; Cisco Agrees To Suspend Patent Suit For 6 Months*, N.Y. Times (Oct. 2, 2003), https://www.nytimes.com/2003/10/02/business/technology-cisco-agrees-to-suspend-patent-suit-for-6-months.html.; In 2014, T-Mobile sued Huawei of photographing and steal-

Where there are challenges, also lie opportunities. Being shut off from the major mobile OS might be detrimental to Huawei's development in the short run, but this forces Huawei to work on a reliable, independent OS of their own. Luckily, Huawei seemingly anticipated such external hostility and was already designing its own HarmonyOS or HongMeng OS since 2021. The external hostility pushed and accelerated this plan - a challenge to Apple's and Google's global duopoly on OS for smartphones.

Huawei may also view this global tension as an opportunity to reflect and revise its operating philosophy. Huawei's motto indeed was to "survive", but as its purview and impact expand, its priority in business strategy and ESG programs may need reassessment and readjustment.

At the end of the day, trust building under multiple cultures with multiple parties of divergent interest pursuit is the surest but most onerous way for Huawei's continued success. During its journey, dedication and commitment to integrity will ultimately disperse prejudice. Huawei's actions and efforts demonstrated a commitment to pursue excellence with integrity. However, Huawei still bears a birthmark of Chinese national origin facing controversially falsified preferences. How China manages to win the trust of the large and divergent global community to brighten the image of all its entities, is a far broader question beyond this article's purview.

---

ing a smartphone-testing robot, Tappy, to help produce Huawei's own robot, resulting in the firing of the alleged Huawei employees, and $4.8 million in damages awarded to T-Mobile. See Hiroko Tabuchi, *T-Mobile Accuses Huawei of Theft From Laboratory*, N.Y. Times (Sept. 5, 2014), https://www.ny-times.com/2014/09/06/business/t-mobile-accuses-huawei-of-theft-from-laboratory.html.

References

Balding, C., & Clarke, D. C. (2019). Who Owns Huawei? https://doi.org/https://dx.doi.org/10.2139/ssrn.3372669

BCG. (2021). *The 50 Most Innovative Companies 2021* Ranking the Brands. https://www.rankingthebrands.com/The-Brand-Rankings.aspx?rankingID=338&year=1367

Bromiley, P., & Harris, J. (2006). Trust, Transaction Cost Economics, and Mechanisms. In *Handbook of Trust Research* (pp. 125-143). Edward Elgar Publishing. https://doi.org/https://doi.org/10.4337/9781847202819.00014

Caldwell, J. H. (2021, February 1). A moving target: Refocusing risk and resiliency amidst continued uncertainty. *Deloitte Insights.* https://www2.deloitte.com/us/en/insights/industry/financial-services/global-risk-management-survey-financial-services.html

CDP. (2021). *Companies scores.* Carbon Disclosure Project. Retrieved January 31 from https://www.cdp.net/en/companies/companies-scores

CDP, CDSB, GRI, IIRC, & SASB. (2020). Statement of intent to work together towards comprehensive corporate reporting: summary of alignment discussions among leading sustainability and integrated reporting organisations CDP, CDSB, GRI, IIRC and SASB. https://29kjwb3armds2g3gi4lq2sx1-wpengine.netdna-ssl.com/wp-content/uploads/Statement-of-Intent-to-Work-Together-Towards-Comprehensive-Corporate-Reporting.pdf

CDSB. (2022). *CDSB Framework for reporting environmental & social information.* Climate Disclosure Standards Board. https://www.cdsb.net/framework

CED Research & Policy Committee. (1971). *Social responsibilities of business corporations.* CED. https://www.ced.org/pdf/Social_Responsibilities_of_Business_Corporations.pdf

China Statistical Yearbook 2021. (2021). China Bureau of Statistics. http://www.stats.gov.cn/tjsj/ndsj/2021/indexeh.htm

Coase, R. H. (1937). The Nature of the Firm. *Economica, 4*(16), 386-405. https://doi.org/https://doi.org/10.1111/j.1468-0335.1937.tb00002.x

Davis, B., & Ferek, K. S. (2020, May 15). U.S. Moves to Cut Off Chip Supplies to Huawei. *The Wall Street Journal.* https://www.wsj.com/articles/u-s-moves-to-cut-off-chip-supplies-to-huawei-11589545335?mod=article_inline

Dyer, J. H., & Chu, W. (2003). The Role of Trustworthiness in Reducing Transaction Costs and Improving Performance: Empirical Evidence from the United States, Japan, and Korea. *Organization Science, 14*(1), 57-68. http://www.jstor.org/stable/3086033

Edelman. (2021a, November 17). *EDELMAN STUDY FINDS CRITICAL NEW DYNAMICS FOR BUILDING TRUST WITH INVESTORS.* Retrieved January 31 from https://www.edelman.com/news-awards/edelman-study-finds-critical-new-dynamics-building-trust-investors

Edelman. (2021b). *WHY TRUST?* Retrieved Jan. 15 from https://www.edelman.com/trust

Edelman. (2022). *2022 Edelman Trust Barometer.* https://www.edelman.com/sites/g/files/aatuss191/files/2022-01/2022%20Edelman%20Trust%20Barometer%20FINAL_Jan25.pdf

Entine, J. (2003). The Myth of Social Investing:A Critique of its Practice and Consequences for Corporate Social Performance Research. *Organization & Environment, 16*(3), 352-368. https://doi.org/10.1177/1086026603256283

European Commission. (2001). *Green paper: Promoting a European framework for corporate social responsibility.* Brussels: Office for Official Publications of the European Communities Retrieved from https://eur-lex.europa.eu/LexUriServ/LexUriServ.do?uri=COM:2001:0366:FIN:EN:PDF

European Commission. (2011). *A renewed EU strategy 2011-14 for corporate social responsibility.* Retrieved from https://eur-lex.europa.eu/legal-content/EN/ALL/?uri=celex:52011DC0681

Flynn, L. J. (2003, October 2). TECHNOLOGY; Cisco Agrees To Suspend Patent Suit For 6 Months. *The New York Times.* https://www.nytimes.com/2003/10/02/business/technology-cisco-agrees-to-suspend-patent-suit-for-6-months.html

Fortune. (2021). *Global 500* Fortune Global 500. https://fortune.com/global500/2020/search/

Friedman, M. (1970, September 13). A Friedman doctrine- The Social Responsibility Of Business Is to Increase Its Profits. *The New York Times.* https://www.nytimes.com/1970/09/13/archives/a-friedman-doctrine-the-social-responsibility-of-business-is-to.html

Goto, T. (2021, May 31). Huawei's Employee Shareholding Scheme: Who Owns Huawei? https://doi.org/http://dx.doi.org/10.2139/ssrn.3856761

GRI. (2021). *GRI 1: Foundation 2021*. Global Reporting Initiative Standards. https://globalreporting.org/pdf.ashx?id=12334&page=9

Henisz, W., Koller, T., & Nuttal, R. (2019, November 14). Five ways that ESG creates value. *McKinsey Quarterly*. https://www.mckinsey.com/business-functions/strategy-and-corporate-finance/our-insights/five-ways-that-esg-creates-value

Hernández-Murillo, R., & Martinek, C. (2009). Corporate Social Responsibility can be profitable. *The Regional Economist*, 4-5. https://www.stlouisfed.org/publications/regional-economist/april-2009/corporate-social-responsibility-can-be-profitable

Huang, Z. (2021, August 26). China Spells Out How Excessive '996' Work Culture is Illegal. *Bloomberg*. https://www.bloomberg.com/news/articles/2021-08-27/china-s-top-court-says-excessive-996-work-culture-is-illegal

Huawei. (2020a). *Annual Report*. https://www-file.huawei.com/minisite/media/annual_report/annual_report_2020_en.pdf

Huawei. (2020b). *Sustainability Report*. https://www-file.huawei.com/-/media/corp2020/pdf/sustainability/sustainability-report-2020-en.pdf

Huawei. (n.d.). *Who Owns Huawei?* Retrieved January 15 from https://www.huawei.com/en/facts/question-answer/who-owns-huawei

IIRC. (2021). International <IR> Framework. In: The International Integrated Reporting Council.

Impact Management Project. (2020, January 31). Statement of intent to work together towards comprehensive corporate reporting. https://impactmanagementproject.com/structured-network/statement-of-intent-to-work-together-towards-comprehensive-corporate-reporting/

Interbrand. (2021). *Best Global Brands 2021* Ranking the Brands. https://www.rankingthebrands.com/The-Brand-Rankings.aspx?rankingID=37

Kappel, M. (2019, April 3). Transparency In Business: 5 Ways to Build Trust. *Forbes*. https://www.forbes.com/sites/mikekappel/2019/04/03/transparency-in-business-5-ways-to-build-trust/?sh=386f29c06149.

Knoepfel, I., & Hagart, G. (2004). *Who Cares Wins: Connecting Financial Markets to a Changing World*. United Nations. https://www.scribd.com/fullscreen/16876740?access_key=key-16pe23pd759qalbnx2pv

Laissez-faire. In. (2019). *Black's Law Dictionary*. https://www.westlaw.com/Document/I01b0638f808511e4b391 a0bc737b01f9/View/FullText.html?transitionType=Default&co ntextData=(sc.Default)&VR=3.0&RS=cblt1.0

Llewellyn, K. N. (1931). What Price Contract?. An Essay in Perspective. *The Yale Law Journal, 40*(5), 704-751. https://doi.org/10.2307/790659

Maimonides, M. (1470). *Mishneh Torah, Laws of Gifts to the Poor* https://www.sefaria.org/Mishneh_Torah%2C_Gifts_to_the_Po or.9.17?ven=Gifts_for_the_Poor,_Trans._by_Joseph_B._Meszl er,_Williamsburg,_Virginia,_2003&vhe=Torat_Emet_363&lan g=en&with=all&lang2=en

McWilliams, A., & Siegel, D. (2001). Corporate Social Responsibility: A Theory of the Firm Perspective. *The Academy of Management Review, 26*(1), 117-127. https://doi.org/10.2307/259398

Murdoch, A. (2021, May 05). ESG reporting confusion hits companies' bottom line. *Capital Monitor*. https://capitalmonitor.ai/institution/investment-managers/esg-reporting-confusion-hits-companies-bottom-line/

Plant, A. (1932). Trends in Business Administration. *Economica*(35), 45-62. https://doi.org/10.2307/2548975

PRI. (2018). *PRI reporting framework main definitions* https://www.unpri.org/Uploads/x/l/q/maindefinitionstoprireport ingframework_971173.pdf

PRI. (n.d.). *What are the Principles for Responsible Investment?* Retrieved February 8 from https://www.unpri.org/about-us/what-are-the-principles-for-responsible-investment

Robertson, D. H. (1936). *The Control of Industry*. University Press.

Rossi, B. (2012, June 12). Huawei and ZTE execs convicted of bribery in Algeria. *Information Age*. https://www.information-age.com/huawei-and-zte-execs-convicted-of-bribery-in-algeria-2107858/

Sarbanes-Oxley Act of 2002, H.R. 3763, 107th Congress (2002). https://www.congress.gov/bill/107th-congress/house-bill/3763/text

Shepardson, D., Freifeld, K., & Alper, A. (2020, May 15). U.S. moves to cut Huawei off from global chip suppliers as China eyes retaliation. *Reuters*. https://www.reuters.com/article/us-usa-huawei-tech-exclusive/u-s-moves-to-cut-huawei-off-from-global-chip-suppliers-as-china-eyes-retaliation-idUSKBN22R1KC

Sridhar, K. (2021, June 14). ESG – What does it mean? *Pro Bono News.* https://probonoaustralia.com.au/news/2021/06/esg-what-does-it-mean/

Tabuchi, H. (2014, September 5). T-Mobile Accuses Huawei of Theft From Laboratory. *The New York Times.* https://www.nytimes.com/2014/09/06/business/t-mobile-accuses-huawei-of-theft-from-laboratory.html

UN Global Compact. (n.d.). United Nations Global Compact. Retrieved February 14 from https://www.unglobalcompact.org

Usher, A. P. (1920). *An Introduction to the Industrial History of England.* Houghton Mifflin. https://books.google.com/books?id=pCMEAAAAMAAJ

von Hayek, F. A. (1933). The Trend of Economic Thinking. *Economica*(40), 121-137. https://doi.org/10.2307/2548761

Whalen, J. (2021, March 31). U.S. campaign against Huawei appears to be working, as Chinese tech giant loses sales outside its home market. *The Washington Post.* https://www.washingtonpost.com/technology/2021/03/31/impact-us-campaign-against-huawei/

Williams, C. (2014, October 9). Huawei is first Chinese brand to break into global top 100. *The Telegraph.* http://www.telegraph.co.uk/finance/newsbysector/mediatechnologyandtelecoms/telecoms/11151842/Huawei-is-first-Chinese-brand-to-break-into-global-top-100.html

Wood, D. J. (1991). Corporate Social Performance Revisited. *The Academy of Management Review, 16*(4), 691-718. https://doi.org/10.2307/258977

World Bank. (2021). *Gross domestic product 2020* World Development Indicators. https://databank.worldbank.org/data/download/GDP.pdf

Xin, H. (2021, August 22). Liubumen lianhe yinfa zhidao yijian zhizaoye youzhi qiye zheyang peiyang. *People's Daily.* http://www.gov.cn/zhengce/2021-08/22/content_5632615.htm

Zhong, R. (2018, December 18). Huawei's 'Wolf Culture' Helped It Grow, and Got It Into Trouble. *The New York Times.* https://www.nytimes.com/2018/12/18/technology/huawei-workers-iran-sanctions.html

2

AMERICAN EXCEPTIONALISM: PRIDE, POWER AND PREJUDICE

Einar Tangen

How the US lost its moral, legal and ethical center after winning the Cold War, and how the new norms of immoral, illegal and unethical actions are affecting the world.[1]

2.1 Introduction

The fall of the Berlin Wall, and the collapse of the USSR, was one of America's proudest moments. Our Cold War ideological foe was vanquished, America's mix of democracy and capitalism reigned supreme,

---

[1] Einar Tangen J.D., Economic and Political Affairs Commentator at CCTV, CGTN, CRI, China.org.cn, Xinhua, Al Jazeera, Press TV, TRT World, CNN News 18, etc. Founder and Chairman of China Cities Bluebook Consulting and Principal of DGI/SMP DESIGN. First published in China-US Focus, https://www.chinausfocus.com/society-culture/american-exceptionalism-pride-power-and-prejudice, 15 October, 2020.

China was barely a blip in the rear view mirror, and the US was the world's sole superpower.

But, the sudden victory was a surprise; there had been little time to work through expectations. The sharp ideological lines of the Cold War which had reminded us of the differences between "us" and "them" melted away, leaving no meaningful guard rails. In essence, the world was ours, the question was, what we should, and would, do with it.

Triumph always has its heralds. For America, it was Francis Fukuyama, fresh from a stint in the Reagan White House, penned an essay "The End of History" (1989), calling for a monochromatic world order based on the victorious US model. Subsequently, the essay was turned into a book: The End of History and the Last Man (1992), which portrayed American Exceptionalism as the logical and inevitable end of political and economic evolution. The term became a rallying cry to bring all countries into an American norm. In doing so, it simultaneously forgave America for its past, and future sins - the "greater good" had required a few broken eggs in the past, and might require a few more in the future. The "ends would justify the means", was the essence of the argument, because the United States was a moral and ethical flagship that sailed under the "rule of law". Ironically, few recognized this massive hypocrisy, in their rush to proselytize their ideology.

Thus began America's journey down the path of good intentions. America is now at a point, under President Donald Trump, where morality, ethics and the rule of law have been sacrificed to political and economic expediency. Morality has become a sop for "suckers" and the Rule of Law has become "rule by law", heralding a new type of "thug politics".

Under Trump's roaring America Firstism, it is no longer about what is good, simply what is good for America.

Many factors contributed to this devolution: the greed and arrogance of elites who let the mainstay of America's stability, the middle class, dwindle and slide into discontent; military adventures that yielded only dead bodies, excessive expenditure that added trillions in debt; a system of government unable to produce responsive and effective leaders; an economic system which has enlarged the wealth gap by bailing out the "too big to fail" companies and their executives, while ordinary people lost their jobs, businesses, pensions and homes; a hot and cold neo-isolationism foreign policy that has rapidly eroded America's international soft power stature.

We have traveled far from the initial euphoria of victory, forty years ago, when democracy, capitalism, multilateral institutions and cooperation were the ideals.

Today, many people feel that freedom is a right that has no corresponding responsibilities, from blaming partners for its own trade defi-cits, to refusing to wear a mask during a pandemic.

Democracy, which depends on a measure of altruism to succeed, has descended into "identity" and "my needs" politics that prohibit rational discussion over issues like abortion, guns, LGBT, race etc...

Capitalism, rather than creating fairer and more efficient markets, has become a tool of inequality, economically and legally. The wealth of the four richest people in the U.S. matches the worth of the bottom 50%.

Multilateral institutions, like the UN, WTO, ICC, WHO, are under attack by the very government, which envisioned and set them up.

Cooperation has been replaced by "thug politics", where the strong take from, or impose on, the weak, using unilateral tariffs, sanctions, military action and political pressure.

Treaty obligations are optional, climate change and pandemics can be ignored and the law simply becomes an enforcement tool for the interests of those in power.

The U.S. is still the most powerful political, economic and military power in the world. Nevertheless, it's "lead by example" and aspirational politics, have given way to a culture of grievance and selfishness - one that blames domestic failures on "them", creates wild conspiratorial theories, fuels a growing sense that America, the victor of the Cold War and defender of the future, has somehow been cheated by its neighbors, allies and the rest of the world.

Under it all, there is an ever-growing existential unease over the rise and success of China, under its hybrid political and economic institutions, which deviates from the gospel of American Exceptionalism.

China's success, contrasted with the failures of the "superior" American system, is the constant, in the deteriorating Sino-US relations. It is the rationalization for aggressive, but largely unsubstantiated, US accusations of cheating, theft and malevolent intent that are leveled on a daily basis against China. It is the basis of US grievances, paranoia, racism and ultimately, the catchall reason for why China is always at fault.

This article is titled Pride, Power and Prejudice, because we are at an inflection point where we will either recover our collective morality, ethics, regard for the rule of law, multilateralism and cooperation, or descend into a maelstrom of "might makes right" politics.

How did we get here? What have been the ramifications to the rule of law and those who seek its protection? It is hoped that the subject of this essay may stir some vigorous debate and some possible answers.

2.2 Pride

With the ascendancy of Western liberal democracy - which occurred after the Cold War (1945–1991) and the dissolution of the Soviet Union (1991) - humanity has reached a point "not just ... the passing of a particular period of post-war history, but the end of history as such:

That is, the end-point of mankind's ideological evolution and the universalization of Western liberal democracy as the final form of human government."[2]

On November 3rd, 1980, President Ronald Reagan, portrayed the United States as "a shining city on a hill whose beacon light guides freedom-loving people everywhere". Subsequently, in 1987, Reagan made his "tear down the wall" speech in Germany, marking the end of the USSR and paving a way for the reunification of Germany.

Ironically, these words and the events, which accompanied them, marked the bookends of a presidency, where the rhetoric and reality were in constant conflict. A presidency where the United States was shedding the moral, legal and ethical ideals, which had since WWII, cast it, despite wars in Korea and Vietnam, political assassinations and continual interference in the affairs of other sovereign nations, as aspirational.

Reagan's Presidency, despite the inspiring words and images, was the beginning of a return to a form of unbridled Realpolitik based on the notion of American Exceptionalism - a concept that freed the U.S. from any moral, legal or ethical constraints. The concept of American Exceptionalism so inspired, is now a rationalization for any means or methods necessary, in pursuit of the "greater good" of imposing Liberal Democratic Capitalism on the entire world.

His presidency was unique in the number, and depth, of scandals, including Iran Contra, the invasion of Granada, the Savings and Loan crisis and the investigation, indictment and conviction of over 138 of his administration's officials, still the largest number for any U.S. President.

This sense of "manifest destiny", defined in "The End of History and the Last Man" (1992) by Francis Fukuyama, proposed that with the ascendancy of Western liberal democracy, as the dominant power, at the end of the Cold War, humanity had reached "not just ... the passing of a

---

[2] Wikipedia, *The End of Histroy and the Last Man*, https://en.m.wikipedia.org/wiki/The_End_of_History_and_the_Last_Man.

particular period of post-war history, but the end of history as such, in essence the finale of mankind's ideological evolution."

Drawn from Fukuyama's 1989 essay, "The End of History?", his grand vision, ironically, based on the linear advancement theories of Hegel and Marx, has since become the battle cry of American Exceptionalists; those who put their faith in the belief that the U.S. possesses a unique, superior society that has a duty to impose its ideological and economic model on the world.

40 years latter any veneer of altruism, that the U.S. had left, is gone. President Trump's "America First" campaign and actions have completed the degradation of any moral, legal and ethical norms, which supposedly differentiated American Liberal Democratic Capitalism from the autocratic systems it says it opposes.

2.3 Power

The heart of this recent hubris is not about confidence, but fear and uncertainty masked by bravado and ideological self-righteousness.

In retrospect, from a revolutionary new nation that willingly turned its back on the "old world" in favor of a new form of enlightened democracy, the U.S. was forced to abandon its isolationism by its growing trade footprint, and two world wars.

Governance in the initial 13 colonies was a pragmatic affair, balancing free men and slaves, different religions, diverse ethnicities, the relationship between the individual and the state and tensions between the 13 states themselves. It brought forth the US Constitution and its Bill of Rights, which while clothed in the rhetoric of the Enlightenment, in reality dealt with the pragmatic realities mentioned above.

Following WWII the desire was to create a more stable world using multilateral political and financial institutions, like the United Nations, World Bank and IMF, as a means of preventing wars in the future - "talks rather than tanks". This was the beginning of the American Century, the expansion of US's diplomatic, trade and security footprint to every corner of the globe.

It also brought to the fore the schism that has been simmering since the widespread of democracy and advent of capitalism. Democracy and Capitalism are processes, not ideologies, like Socialism or Communism. As processes, they describe what is perceived to be a more efficient way of governance and economics. The rationales are that Democracy allows voters to remove inefficient leaders and governments, and Capitalism employs the power of the market to remove inefficient managers and companies.

The reality for America is, its two-party democracy, which held captive by local issues and special interests, has failed to give US voters efficient leaders or responsive governments. The "free market" capitalists, who proselytize the gospel of the "Chicago School"; that free markets best allocate resources in an economy and that minimal, or even no, government intervention is best for economic prosperity, have not allocated resources efficiently, instead creating monopolies and oligarchies that dominates almost every industry, enriching their owners at the expense of their workers. Add in a world where the lion's share of corporate profits between 2000 and 2018 went to developed nations, which was reflected in the almost tripling of US corporate profits.

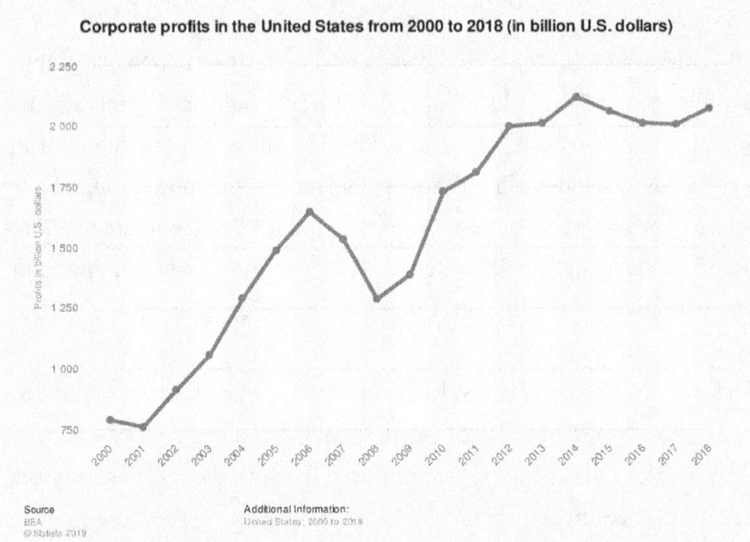

Figure 1: Corporate profits in the United States from 2000 to 2018 (billion USD). Source: BEA, Statista 2019.

At this was happening, the US GDP doubled, from 10 to 20 trillion dollars, but not the income or numbers of middle class Americans, which deteriorated.[3]

"Income and class position over two fifteen-year periods (1967 to 1981 and from 2002 to 2016). Specifically, for individuals aged 25 to 44 at the start of these periods, using data from the Panel Study on Income Dynamics (PSID), comparing the two periods, the main findings are as follows:

The median income growth experienced by prime-age Americans over a fifteen-year period has been cut by almost two thirds, from 27% to 8%. The proportion experiencing a large income loss has more than tripled, from 4% to 12%. The upper middle class has expanded significantly,

---

[3] Kimberly Amadeo (2022). U.S. GDP by Year, Compared to Recessions and Event, the Balance, https://www.thebalance.com/us-gdp-by-year-3305543changes.

while the "middle" middle class (MMC) has shrunk from 50% to 36%. Income growth at the top of the distribution has been almost twice as fast as in the middle (48% at the 95th percentile, compared to 26% at the median). Upward mobility out of poverty has declined, from 43% to 35%. Downward mobility from the MMC has doubled, from 5% to 11%. The proportion of Black Americans in the upper middle class has increased significantly, from just 1% to 14%. Nevertheless, large race gaps remain: 39% of whites are in the upper middle class or higher. More education has become more closely associated with a higher income; 59% of those with a BA+ are in the upper middle class or higher, up from 37%."[4]

The greatest subconscious fear that the American establishment has, is that its facade of contradictions will be unmasked. The result has been an emphasis on an ever growing self-righteous proselytizing based on the neo-fascist "manifest destiny" of American Exceptionalism. The apex of this trend has been the election of Donald Trump, who presents American Exceptionalism at its ugliest. The pathological lies, the constant boasting, the lack of empathy, the disregard for personal, business, social, political and international norms, morality, laws and ethics, have become the domestic and international face of America.

Under Donald Trump, power is a tool that allows the U.S. to impose its policies and interests on other countries. Morality is not a factor; children can be taken from their mothers and deported without their parents, dictators can be supported when there is a personal, political or financial interest, pressing human needs, like poverty, pandemics, climate change, can be ignored.

For him, legality does not matter, the law is a means of exercising power over, not protecting, the powerless. Unilateral economic, political

---

[4] Stephen Rose (2020). Squeezing the middle class: income trajectories from 1967 to 2016, Brookings Report, https://www.brookings.edu/research/squeezing-the-middle-class/#:~:text=The%20upper%20middle%20class%20has,26%25%20at%20the%20median.

and military actions are implemented based on archaic laws left over from the Cold War. Neighbors, allies, and competitors are treated with equal disdain in pursuit of putting "America First".

But of all the actions, the most significant and telling are those against China. Attacks on Chinese tech companies, including Huawei, ZTE, Tik-Tok, WeChat and many other leading tech firms are justified by repetitive unproven claims and political pressure.

In terms of Tiktok, the legal basis for the unilateral action was about what might happen, not one shred of proof that anything actually had happened.

Unsurprisingly the US courts imposed a stay based on the probable violations of Free Speech and Due Process under the US Constitution. The list goes on: the withdrawal from the Paris Climate Accord, TPP, WTO, UNESCO, JPCOA, Chinese Media restrictions, personal sanctions of Chinese government officials, stirring discontent in HK, Taiwan, Xinjiang, Tibet, India, and ASEAN.

Domestically, the Trump administration uses the law to pursue his political and personal agendas. Politically, he has tried to extend the power of Executive Orders beyond any constitutional norm, as witnessed by the string of legal defeats his administration has suffered on issues like DACA and the Citizen Census Question. In terms of his personal interests, the Attorney General has become the protector of his and his allies' interests. Jeff Sessions was ostracized and humiliated for not preventing the impeachment proceedings despite his clear legal and ethical conflicts. Barr has become his watchdog, allowing Trump's Washington hotel to operate despite the emoluments clause, allowing the Department of Justice to defend Trump's refusal to turn over his tax returns, defending the President's sexual molestation cases, supporting the commutation and pardons of those with connections to the President and his family, like Rodger Stone, Michael Flynn, the removal of prosecutors and interference in their investigations, the removal of Inspector General's whose investigations come to close to the President. The list goes on.[5]

Without morals or regard for the rule of law, ethics is meaningless, so the lack of personal or professional ethics of Trump and his administration, while grievous by normal standards, is, in a Trumpian universe, simply normal behaviors.[6]

The net effect has been to make the US more unpopular.

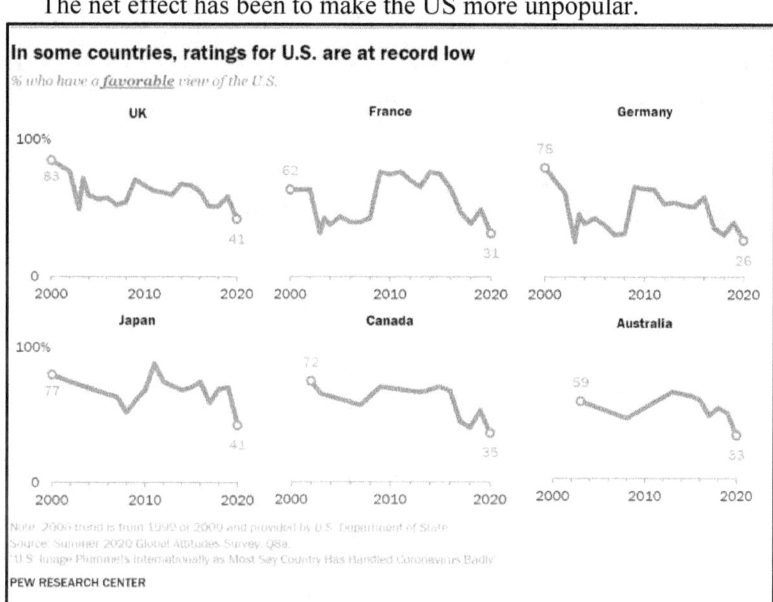

Figure 2: Record low ratings for U.S. in some countries

---

[5] Ben Parker, Stephanie Steinbrecher, Kelsey Ronan, John Mcmurtrie, Sophia Durose, Rachel Villa, and Amy Sumerton (2021). *Lest We Forget The Horrors: A Catalog Of Trump'S Worst Cruelties, Collusions, Corruptions, and Crimes.* McSWEENEY's, https://www.mcsweeneys.net/articles/the-complete-listing-atrocities-1-1-056.

[6] Sheng Lu (2021). FASH455 *Global Apparel & Textile Trade and Sourcing.* Shenglufashion.com, https://shenglufashion.com/timeline-of-trade-policy-in-the-trump-administration/.

Source: Summer 2020 Global Attitudes Survey, Pew Research Center, https://www.pewresearch.org/global/2020/09/15/us-image-plummets-internationally-as-most-say-country-has-handled-coronavirus-badly/

The mixture of pride and power has taken the U.S. down a dark road, where it has abandoned any semblance of morality, ethics or respect for the rule of law. It is now consumed with proving itself the "better country", unfortunately, as its efforts backfire and China continues to prosper, Washington's efforts are getting more manic, merging political, economic and military containment efforts.

China's success is an existential threat to those who believe in the absolute certainty of American Exceptionalism and Fukuyama's "End of History". To Trump and the China Hawks in his administration, China is the visible red flag.

2.4 Prejudice

Many westerners do not take Asians seriously. The attacks on Chinese technology implies a conception that Asians are incapable of inventing a leading technology without copying or cheating. The subtext is both racial and nationalistic. How could Chinese companies, under a centrally led socialist government, achieve innovation ahead of a white led Western Liberal Democratic Capitalist country? So, a Chinese company couldn't possibly develop 5G in advance of the U.S. without stealing and cheating. Interestingly, it is what the British said about Americans during the late 1800's. The embedded conviction is that Asians, like Hispanics, Blacks, other minorities and women are inferior to whites.

In terms of Covid-19, many in the West saw it, and still see it, in terms of ethnocentric racial and cultural stereotyping - the superior white, liberal democratic capitalist countries, must by definition, enjoy the upper hand in crisis management - therefore, it is inconceivable that China has been able to bring the coronavirus under far better control than their "superiors". The only explanation left is that China must have either falsified its data or it was all a sinister plot.

This, in turn, has led to a teachable moment for Asians, as many of these "superior" countries struggle with their pandemic responses. Confidence in the country and the central government, which has always been high[7], is now growing[8].

In contrast, foreign and domestic approval of the U.S., which has been historically low, except before wars, has recently gone even lower. (See same sources as quoted above).

Trump's campaign promise was to "Make America Great Again", unfortunately his idea is based on a past dominated by white men that is extremely problematic and "tone deaf" for minorities, women and others struggling with prejudice.

At an ABC Town Hall meeting on September 16th, 2020 Trump was asked by Carl Day: "When has America been great for African Americans in the ghetto of America?"… "Are you aware of how tone-deaf that comes off to the African American community?" Trump's response was to indicate he has "tremendous" support in the black community, itself a fabrication, since he only received 8% of the Black vote in 2016.

The larger point is that his non-answer combined with his statements and business practices, listed in Wikipedia, confirms the absence of moral, ethical or legal regard for minorities or women.[9]

---

[7] Dan Harsha (2020). *Taking China's pulse*, the Harvard Gazette, https://news.harvard.edu/gazette/story/2020/07/long-term-survey-reveals-chinese-government-satisfaction/

[8] Xinhua (2020). *Global survey: China continues to win high public confidence*, Xinhua Net, http://www.xinhuanet.com/english/2020-03/04/c_138843729.htm

[9] Wikipedia. Racial views of Donald Trump, https://en.m.wikipedia.org/wiki/Racial_views_of_Donald_Trump

2.5 Conclusion

China's unforgivable sin, in American eyes, is its success. It is inconceivable to many Americans, like Trump, that a nation with a different political and economic system, could, for example, surpass America, in a critical industry like 5G, or challenge America's political, economic and military hegemony. If you have the only solution, there can be no other solution. For the people who believe this, the only solution is to put "these people back in their place", before they mislead others.

The "dark road" of American Exceptionalism, embraced by many in the US, is based on pride, power and prejudice and is removing the fundamental American moral, ethical and legal signposts upon which the nation was founded in favor of political and economic expediency. Let us hope that through reflection, or experience, this will change.

3

AMERICAN EXCEPTIONALISM: LAND, DESTINY AND VIRTUE

Heidi Hadsell

Ideas, which serve as important elements of national identity, circulate within every nation.[1] These ideas are both implicit and explicit, and they may be fully noticed by only a few but they are shared by many. Together these ideas are elements that compose a story of self-understanding that that nation shares about itself to its own citizens and to outsiders. The narrative includes an interpretation of the history of that nation, its aspirations, values, practices, rituals and the like, through which it defines itself, and also through which it defines its difference from other nations. This kind of national narrative serves to bring disparate groups and interests within a given nation together, and also serves to invoke and encourage common pride and a shared sense of belonging. In this sense President Obama was quite correct when, asked by a journalist about American exceptionalism, he answered that every nation thinks of itself as exceptional.

---

[1] Prof. Dr. Heidi Hadsell, Prof em. of Ethics and former President of Hartford Internat. University for Religion and Peace, San Francisco, USA.

He then went on to list the values, laws, beliefs and practices that in his view make America exceptional:

3.1 The new Land

"I believe in American exceptionalism, just as I suspect that the Brits believe in British exceptionalism and the Greeks believe in Greek exceptionalism. I am enormously proud of my country and its role and history in the world… And I think we have a core set of values that are enshrined in our Constitution, in our body of laws, in our democratic practices, in our belief in free speech and equality that, though imperfect, are exceptional."[2]

Obama's use of the term 'exceptional' refers broadly to the set of shared beliefs, practices, institutions, values, rituals, which together the philosopher Charles Taylor very helpfully calls the 'social imaginary,' of a given people.[3]

The social imaginary of which American exceptionalism is a part and which is widely shared by many of the American people has many sources. The earliest historical sources date back to the very early days of the first years of the European settlers on the new soil, and have to do with their perception of the unique nature of the land that was to be their new home. The early European settlers viewed this land, which was for them a recent discovery, as largely untouched and empty, fertile and full of potential, and thus in many ways entirely different from the land from which they came. This perception, this myth, of the land as empty and essentially free for the taking of it, ignored or greatly minimized, the presence of the native peoples across the continent, who the settlers fought and killed in order to seize their land.

---

[2] April 4, 2009, press conference in Strasbourg, France

[3] See for example *A Secular Age*. The Belknap Press of Harvard University Press, Cambridge, Massachusetts and London, England, 2007.

In the eyes of the early Europeans settlers this new and fertile land represented the chance for them to begin again. For many it was a chance to escape from the existing political, economic and social structures in the lands from which they came, and thus it represented the freedom to pursue opportunities that would have been far beyond their reach in their countries of origin. For others such as the early Protestant Puritans, the uniqueness of this new land also represented the opportunity to escape from the religious tyranny of their native lands, and they rejoiced in their newfound freedom to practice their own religion as they wished.

Many of the early settlers were Puritans and their worldview was such that they saw this new land and themselves in this new land religiously – that is, they saw the land, and their presence on it as part of God's will, or, in their vocabulary, part of "divine providence". The Puritans viewed themselves as divinely blessed by God who had brought them to this new land.

In the Puritan understanding, the covenant they shared with God, which had brought so many blessings, carried not only untold blessings, but also clear obligations. The obligations for the Puritans included the duty to act with special virtue, to create civic organizations that would serve as a civic model for others, to construct a country that would serve as a beacon, a "city on a hill" for all to see.

"For we must consider that we shall be as a city upon a hill. The eyes of all people are upon us. So that if we shall deal falsely with our God in this work we have undertaken, and so cause Him to withdraw His present help from us, we shall be made a story and a by-word through the world."[4]

The American sociologist Robert Bellah writing in the 20th century on what he called the 'civil religion' in America, underlined the danger inherent in identifying good fortune with God's will, and thus the importance of the internalized moral obligations of the nation. Bellah comments:

---

[4] John Winthrop (1630), *Dreams of a City on a Hill.*

"Without an awareness that our nation stands under judgment, the tradition of the civil religion would be dangerous indeed. Fortunately, the prophetic voices have never been lacking."[5]

3.2 A special destiny and virtue

In many expressions of American exceptionalism today one can still find important echoes of this sense of America having a special *destiny*, but also in some way special responsibility. In many other expressions of contemporary American exceptionalism however, the importance of civic and national self-critique which was part of the inner moral logic of Puritan Christianity is entirely absent.

As history demonstrates, this claim of, or hope for, special moral virtue and reward, was asserted by the Puritans despite their living in the context of the on-going and devastating wars of the settlers against the native peoples, and their theft of native lands. The claim of special moral virtue persisted through the revolutionary war and also persisted through the massive, violent, theft, murder, and transportation of many thousands of African peoples from Africa to American soil for their enslavement on that soil which lasted close to 100 years.

The violence, the murder and the subjugation of the First Peoples and of African peoples, were brutal empirical facts that clearly negated the claims of those who saw themselves or saw their new country as somehow morally exceptional. Paradoxically however, for some, the claims of their own moral exceptionalism and the claim of the collective moral exceptionalism of white settlers in general, helped serve to justify this violent reality. It reassured those who greatly benefitted from and participated in slavery, and the subjugation of First Peoples, in the face of clear evidence to the contrary, that their economic success proved somehow that they were morally correct or superior.

---

[5] Winter Daedalus (1967), *Civil Religion in America*.

In his Annual Message to Congress, on Dec 1,1862, a month before he signed the Emancipation Proclamation which formally ended slavery in the United States, Lincoln acknowledged the evil of slavery, and the importance of ending it, even as he also acknowledged what he saw as the exceptional nature of the United States, calling it "the last best hope of earth."

"…We say we are for the Union. The world will not forget that we say this. We know how to save the Union. The world knows we do know how to save it. We - even we here - hold the power and bear the responsibility. In giving freedom to the slave, we assure freedom to the free - honorable alike in what we give, and what we preserve. We shall nobly save, or meanly lose, the last best hope of earth. Other means may succeed; this could not fail. The way is plain, generous, just - a way which, if followed, the world will forever applaud, and God must forever bless.[6]

The American revolution has been an enduring and important reference for American exceptionalism and along with it, the creation of the Constitution of the United States of America, and the institutions and practices of representative democracy. The founding of the United States of America and the formation of American democratic political and legal institutions, which were at that time, in many ways unique, were and continue to be a source of great shared civic pride and have contributed significantly to a shared sense among Americans of being different.

Today, as at many other times in American history, the political left and the political right, when they cannot agree upon anything else, or little else, often still turn to their common commitment to and shared pride in the democratic practices and institutions of the United States. Part of their shared conviction is that the United States democracy is a model that others can and should learn from. The shared belief in American democratic

---

[6] *President Lincoln's Annual Address to Congress*, Dec. 1, 1862, Washington D.C.

institutional uniqueness has been an important contributor to internal unity despite political and other differences

3.4 Criticism of exceptionalism as hypocrisy

While the claims of American exceptionalism have often been broadly shared in American history and widely taught across the society, it is also the case that strong resistance to and critiques of American exceptionalism are also a long-standing part of the American social imaginary. There are numerous moments in American history in which one can see clearly these two contradictory positions regarding American exceptionalism which coexist in the social imaginary, come into open tension and overt conflict with each other. The period of the war in Viet Nam was one such era.

The moral justification to the American people for involvement in the Viet Nam war by American political authorities, often downplayed the self-interest of the US government and American companies, and instead emphasized the position that the war was for the benefit of the Vietnamese people, who sought the sort of democracy and economic freedom that one finds in the United States, and other arguments along the same line.

Some Americans, primarily on the left, were against the war from the very beginning, and as the war progressed, while many continued to support it, growing numbers of people met the claims of the US government of moral altruism with disgust and derision, and countered the claims with furious accusations of hypocrisy and imperialism. Young men resisted the draft, individual religious groups and national denominations as well as many other civic institutions and organizations turned or already were against the war, demonstrations were ubiquitous and the streets rang with chants such as "Hey, Hey LBJ, How Many Kids did you Kill Today?" Well before it ended, a significant sector of the American people, and especially the American youth were bitterly opposed to the war and to the national leaders who defended and perpetrated it.

The Viet Nam war left an indelible mark on the nation and especially on the youth of the nation who had become aware of the role the ideas of American exceptionalism played in the selling of the war to the American people, while masking the reality of all the ways that the war was really about American militarism abroad. Many in the United States since the Viet Nam war have remained suspicious of the claims of American exceptionalism. These critics join those who came before them who have over the centuries in one way or another protested against, and worked against the idea of the assertion of American exceptionalism at home or in the international arena.

American exceptionalism has been questioned since its inception from many different directions by many Americans. In 1980 the historian and political scientist Howard Zinn published a book entitled "The People's History of the United States," which recounted American history, but from the perspective of workers, immigrants, African Americans, Japanese Americans who had spent World War Two in internment camps and others. The book was met with great interest especially from younger Americans. These Americans have also welcomed and learned from African American historians and social scientists, poets and literary authors who study the slave trade and slavery or the period of re-construction, segregation or Black experience in contemporary society, and who are joined by Native American colleagues who write and speak from their own experience, and many others who offer profound critiques of American exceptionalism based on the historical and lived reality within the very diverse American society. As a result, the awareness of the hypocrisy of much of the claims of American exceptionalism is high among many Americans today, especially the younger Americans.

3.5 Chastened American exceptionalism

The presidency of Donald Trump, who during his presidency ignored and felt constrained by the nation's democratic institutions, and who disdained any commitment to them, has eroded considerably the pride that had been shared across the political spectrum in American political and civic institutions. In addition, Trump's presidency has made many in the United States rethink how strong or how fragile the institutions themselves have become and question how committed some Americans really are to their endurance.

The claim of, or assurance of the American possession of special institutions, and special virtue as well as the unique nature of the land on which they are found, was for many years internalized and shared by many if not most Americans as part of the American social imaginary. As such it has served as an important source to draw on for leaders through the years. These leaders have been able to appeal to these convictions and emotions and use them to motivate people to uncritically support actions of the US government, even actions which, for example in some American military incursions abroad, might perhaps not have been well supported otherwise.

Today the home of this kind of American exceptionalism is largely found in the American political right. This kind of American exceptionalism prides itself on its patriotism, and tends to regard any critique of American actions abroad as unpatriotic. This perspective is especially prominent in the political thought of American Republicans. The title of former Vice President Dick Cheney's book, published in 2015, expresses the philosophy of the political right very well. The title is: "Exceptional: Why the World needs a Powerful America."

The journalist Peter Beinart described the moment we are in well, and very succinctly when he observed in 2019: "On this July 4, the American left and right, which disagree on almost everything, are both turning against American exceptionalism. Democrats don't think America lives up to liberal democratic ideals. Republicans don't think Americans need to."[7]

On January 20, 2021, President Biden delivered his inaugural address to the American people. In the speech one hears clear echoes of the kind of exceptionalism the American people still expect to hear at such moments. Importantly however, Biden tempers the rhetoric of exceptionalism somewhat with his public recognition of the very slow pace of progress towards the country living up to its ideals. The speech is written in this way certainly because Biden (and his speechwriters) know that many long to hear the high notes of American exceptionalism on such public and important occasions. But they clearly also know that many others long to hear a realistic critique of an American exceptionalism they no longer believe in and a realistic assessment of the nation's strengths and weaknesses. In his speech Biden said: "I know the forces that divide us are deep and they are real, but I also know that they are not new. Our history has been a constant struggle between the American ideal that we're all created equal and the harsh, ugly reality that racism, nativism, fear, demonization have long torn us apart. The battle is perennial and victory is never assured."[8]

The Trump presidency, the rise of the radical right and its distrust of and manipulation of American institutions, the badly handled national response to Covid-19 and the more than 500,000 who have died, together with the sharpening ideological divisions within the American society, all suggest that the United States is actually not exceptional in the ways it has claimed to be. Thus it seems safe to say that going forward, the appeal to and enthusiasm for American exceptionalism, will be much chastened, at least for many Americans.

---

[7] Peter Beinart (2019), *The Left and the Right Have Abandoned American Exceptionalism*. The Atlantic Magazine, July 14, 2019.

[8] *President Biden's Inaugural address*, January 20, 2021.

4

EXCEPTIONALISMS WORLDWIDE: GLOBAL ETHICS AS A RESPONSE

Christoph Stückelberger

American exceptionalism is the predominant topic of this book.[1] In this contribution, I place the exceptionalism of one superpower in the context of other exceptionalisms, which exist across the globe and across history, in empires and in small states, religiously motivated or in secular form. At the same time, each concept – I would call it ideology – of exceptionalism has its historical, geographic, economic and religious specificities. The perspective of a global ethics across nations, cultures and religions includes a fundamental critique of exceptionality and offers in re-placement the vision that we all are exceptional in our own rights and this uniqueness contributes to the beauty, diversity and unity of humanity and the whole creation. This global ethics perspective with its four ethical responses below is concluded by the religious perspective: we can put exceptionalism in the right place by acknowledging that there is only one truly exceptional entity: the Divine, in China called Heaven.

---

[1] Prof. Dr Dr h.c. Christoph Stückelberger, Professor of Ethics (emeritus in Basel), Visiting Prof in China, Russia, UK, Nigeria. Founder and President of Globethics.net and other not-for-profit global foundations.

4.1 Characteristics of exceptionalism

Exceptionalism is the worldview that a nation, ethnic group, people (Volk), family, religion, individual or society is extraordinary in its qualities and mission in the world. Exceptionalism has existed in many nations throughout history such as the ancient Rome, ancient Greece, ancient India and the Ottoman Empire. In modern times, the worldview of exceptionalism persists but with different intensity – evident in the United States, Australia, France, Germany under Hitler, India, Pakistan, Imperial Japan, Iran, Serbia, Israel, North Korea, South Africa under Apartheid, the imperial Spain, imperial Great Britain, Russia and more.[2]

Exceptionalism is characterized by an attitude and belief of superiority of one's own nation, group, or religion over all others. It is an expression of nationalism and of imperialism in the case of powerful countries. In religious perspective, the concept of the 'chosen people' as a special mandate and mission from God is prevalent. Exceptionalism is also at the root of racism and apartheid. Historical justifications, often by an origin myth of one's own history, culture and religion, offer the cement for unity.

Exceptionalism can create a strong identity among the people included. In addition, the identity forged through unity is also reached through the exclusion of others, e.g. white supremacy over non-white citizens, the Rus (Russian ethnic group) as the true Russians and the Han as the true Chinese.

As exceptionalism has existed throughout history and continents, it seems exceptionalism as a worldview is not an exceptional and unique perspective! As a result, nations who claim to be exceptional fight other nations who also claim to be exceptional to assert their supremacy. Therefore, exceptionalism is one justification for warfare. Defeating exceptionalism is key for peace.

---

[2] For literature for these countries see https://en.wikipedia.org/wiki/Exceptionalism#History.

4.2 American exceptionalisms

American exceptionalism is widespread in the American perception of national identity. At the same time, American exceptionalism is not so exceptional if we look at history and the long list of nations mentioned above. What is specific? I am not specialized in America as other contributors in this collection of articles. However, I have formulated some analysis and observations from the international comparison: American exceptionalism is historically somehow rooted in the American Revolutionary War 1765-1783 in which the American Colonies defeated the British Empire and formed the United States of America, the first modern constitutional liberal democracy. Americans can be proud of this historical contribution to humanity. It influenced the French revolution shortly after in 1789 and many shifts from colonialism and aristocracy to liberal democracy. But is it enough to speak about exceptionalism?

The historic event was cemented by the religious perspective of (white) Americans as the 'chosen people'. The three Abrahamic religions Judaism, Christianity and Islam all have this notion of being selected and called by God for a special mission in this world. This idea of the 'chosen people' often includes an eschatological perspective to save the world until the end of the time. However, the interpretation of 'chosen people' is fundamentally different in the three religions, as we will see later in this article.

The title of this subchapter is "American Exceptionalisms" in plural, as various dimensions and justifications can be distinguished. The first dimension is the above-mentioned origin of exceptionality as the first nation with a liberal democracy and thus missioned (until recently) to bring liberalism and democracy to the whole world. Another aspect is the religious exceptionalism, especially among Evangelical and Pentecostal Christians, who have a combined world mission to convert and baptize as many humans as possible across the globe. A third American exceptionalism is linked to science and technology, where the USA is seen as the spearhead of technological innovation. A fourth form of American exceptionalism can be seen in the anti-racism movements, such as the non-violent civil rights movement of Martin Luther King, that aimed to counteract white supremacy and promote multi-racial tolerant societies that respected human rights for all in America and across the globe.

4.3 Other superpowers' exceptionalisms

Many countries throughout history have an imbedded ideology of exceptionalism in their national narrative. France, Great Britain, Spain, Portugal and the Ottoman Empire had it as colonial superpowers and Empires[3], and such thinking gave them the self-confidence to conquer the world, and build the best navy, strongest political system, richest cultural heritage and language. Huge contributions to world history (like the French revolution) were made - all through belief of a divine calling or being chosen people. Many of these superpowers have been and are global trading nations and powers.[4] Exceptionalism is then linked to expansionism: the will to expand and dominate beyond one's own borders.

China continues to see itself as exceptional due to five thousand years of cultural and intellectual heritage and persistence throughout the long chain of its dynasties. Russia, after the collapse of the Soviet Union, re-emphasized its very old historical identity as a Russian-Orthodox united nation. Russia and the Russian-Orthodox Church celebrated in 1988, a thousand years of the church, remembering the baptism of Vladimir I, ruler of the Kiev Rus. In addition, Russia's size is exceptional, as it is the geographically largest country from Central Europe to Japan. Turkey in various form also sees itself with a historical mission in the world, as a

---

[3] See Stückelberger, Christoph: *Globalance. Ethics Handbook for a Balanced World Post-Covid*, Globethics.net, Geneva 2020, 94-102 on Empires.
[4] Kotkin, Joel, *Stämme der Macht. Der Erfolg weltweiter Clans in Wirtschaft und Politik*, Rowohlt: Reinbek Bei Hamburg, 1996.

leading Islamic country and a bridge between East and West. Iran, with its many thousand-year-old history and centre of both the Shiite part of Islam and a large Persian Empire in the past, also claims an exceptional role in world history. More examples of exceptionalism from world history can be found in the Roman Empire, the Mongol empire, the Byzantine Empire, the Maurya Empire covering India, Pakistan and Afghanistan and more. We can observe that most of the empires – due to their dominance in size, and political, military and technological-economic power – described them-selves as exceptional, although with different meaning.

4.4 Small states' exceptionalisms

However, small states also see themselves as exceptional. The small size of a nation could lead to a minority complex, but another narrative of exceptionalism can develop based on historical, religious, political, racial or innovative grounds. Let us start with my country of origin and residence:

Switzerland is a tiny area in the midst of Europe, which until the 19th century was a developing country with many emigrants due to widespread poverty.[5] In the 20th century, Switzerland saw itself as exceptional, on top in wealth, innovation, financial systems, peace and more. It turned its small size into an advantage: at the crossroads of North and South, East and West in Europe, a historical myth of Wilhelm Tell, the small 'David' conquering the big empires, the uniqueness of Swiss neutrality, of Swiss quality, Swiss work ethics and extraordinary contribution to humanity such as the Swiss founder of the Red Cross Henri Dunant. It was a narrative of Swiss exceptionalism, a secular form of the 'chosen people'

---

[5] *La Suisse, pays en développement.* 1798-1848-1998-2048, Revue Sud 5/1998.

(auserwähltes Volk)[6], which then became, especially after World War II, more and more an ideology. In 1991, the 700-year celebration of the beginning of Switzerland in 1291, an intense debate arose about the identity and self-understanding of Switzerland and its role as an exceptional country in the world. Since then, under conditions of globalization and a certain isolation in Europe as non-member of the European Union, Switzer-land has come back to a more realistic view of having some exceptional characteristics, but is in many aspects a normal country with strengths and weaknesses.

Israel is another example of a small country with the notion of exceptionalism. Again, Israel has an exceptional history as the Jewish people were without a land and nation, suffered an incomparable holocaust and became the scapegoat for many evils such as pandemics throughout centuries. The deeper root of Israeli exceptionalism lies in the religious view of Judaism being the faith of a chosen people. Again, religious narratives like the biblical story of little David (later King David) defeating giant Goliath cemented this view.

What is the ethical response to these manifold national exceptionalisms in a modern globalized and interdependent world? Let me suggest a fourfold answer.

4.5 Ethical response 1: All humans are chosen people

What is the ethical response on the notion of 'chosen people'[7]? As it is a religious perspective, it has to be defeated by a religious perspective in order to convince believers. Let me answer from the Christian perspective of the New Testament. The notion of the 'chosen people' is deeply

---

[6] Zweifel, Harry, *Wir sind ein auserwähltes Volk! Die Schweiz als Vorbild 700jähriger Demokratie und friedvollen Zusammenlebens*, Lantsch-Lenz Biograph, 1999.

[7] https://en.wikipedia.org/wiki/Chosen_people.

rooted in Judaism and its holy scripture the Torah, the Hebrew Old Testament Bible: God selected the Jewish people and gave them a special vocation and calling, fixed in the Divine, the absolute, to play the specific role individually and as a group, thus an Alliance of God with his people. Exceptionalism was often interpreted as the right to dominate and oppress based on superiority, but Old Testament calling was rather an obligation to be obedient and faithful to the one God in response to the faithfulness and protection of God for the chosen people. This alliance includes the obligation to serve the members of the chosen people and to protect especially the weak, as expressed in many books of the Old Testament such as Dtn 26:1-11. Exceptionalism in the ethical sense, is of exceptionally caring people.

Jesus was born a Jew but then enlarged the vision of the 'chosen people' dramatically: chosen is not a matter of blood, ethnicity, tribes, class or status, but the issue of faith alone: anybody who believes in the Kingdom of God, visible in the servant leadership of this poor Jesus, is chosen and thus belongs to the eschatological global community. The revolutionary shift from Judaism to Christianity is that every individual, without limitation, can be part of the 'chosen', called by God to serve. Everybody can thus become 'exceptional'! It is a fundamental 'democratization' or equalization of exceptionalism. It is expressed in a simple and impressive way in the Christian perspective of community of persons with gifts (charism, charisma in New Testament Greek): "There are different kinds of gifts (charisma), but the same spirit. There are different kinds of service, but the same Lord. There are different kinds of working, but the same God works all of them in all men. Now, to each one the manifestation of the Spirit is given for the common good" (Bible, 1 Cor 12:4-7). Some have the gift of knowledge, others of wisdom, others of healing or of prophecy (1 Cor 12:8-11). Each believer/follower of the teaching of Jesus is exceptional in his/her own right with her/his specific gifts. Together they build the community of servants and stewards for humanity and for the common good (Luke 12:45ff). Inclusion instead of exclusion is the result of this vision of 'exceptional' individuals! Therefore, Christians cannot be nationalists or racists, as they are 'people among all people', answering the call to serve wherever they are, as citizens of the Kingdom of God which has a vision for humanity – not primarily as citizens of a nation that claims to be exceptional. We could call it a new exceptionalism as universalism, or as Paul in the letter to the Corinthians proclaimed: we are one body with many parts and gifts (1 Cor 12).

4.6 Ethical response 2: The beauty of plurality of exceptionalisms

This New Testament does not mean that we have to deny exceptionalism completely, but we have to transform it from an ethical perspective: There is not one exceptional nation, race or ethnic group, but there are manifold exceptional individuals, groups, nations and religions. Like a field of beautiful flowers with high biodiversity where each flower is unique and exceptional, the community of nations, races, ethnic groups, languages, cultures, historic pathways, age groups and religions build a unique bouquet of 'flowers', each entity exceptional in its uniqueness. The beauty of the plurality of exceptionalisms leads us to ethical modesty and inclusivity.

4.7 Ethical response 3: Defeating exceptionalism for peace and multilateralism

This new, inclusive understanding of 'exceptionalism' defeats the exclusive exceptionalism and replaces it with multilateralism, equality of nations and peaceful cooperation. Exceptionalism in its above-described ideological form distorts and misinterprets historical facts of a nation by denying that each nation has also weaknesses and is in many aspects, average. A realistic self-understanding of a nation is much more sustainable than this ideological narrative of exceptionalism, which - sooner or later - breaks down and, like all Empires, disappear. Religious and political fundamentalisms[8] and extremisms share with exceptionalism this ideological foundation of exclusion, arrogance, and physical or mental violence. It denies the value of others, leading to lack of respect and lack of recognition[9]. The ethical answer is to be exceptional not at the expense and on the backs of others, but to be exceptional in service, love, respect, humility and gratitude.

4.8 Ethical response 4: Interpreting the Holy Scriptures with spiritual depth

Exceptionalism as well as religious fundamentalism cannot be defeated with secular or humanistic appeals alone. The alternative 'exceptionalism' as a value-system of global ethics and love for humanity as described above can only be persuasive if the Holy Scriptures of the different religions, which are used as justification for exceptionalism and chosen people ideologies, are carefully interpreted with historical-critical methods that contextualize holy texts with spiritual depth in order to show the deeper meaning. This is the reason why serious theological education of pastors, priests, imams and gurus is not just a private affair of the respective religious communities, but a public affair of a nation. Theological faculties in state universities, as it is still the case in many countries in Europe, but rather rare in the Americas, Africa and Asia, can be justified and is absolutely in line with a modern pluralistic and religiously neutral state. The more theological education is integrated in academic pluralistic

---

[8] Hadsell, Heidi/ Stückelberger, Christoph (eds.), *Overcoming Fundamentalism. Ethical Responses from Five Continents*. Globethics.net: Geneva 2009.

[9] Fernando, Joseph I, *Religious Fundamentalism and an Ethics of Recognition*, in Hadsell, Heidi/ Stückelberger, Christoph (eds.), Overcoming Fundamentalism. Ethical Responses from Five Continents. Globethics.net: Geneva 2009, 69-88 (82f).

institutions and the less it is isolated in closed seminaries, Islamic schools or Buddhist and Hindu monasteries, the more likely it is that fundamentalisms, extremisms and exceptionalisms can grow. It is therefore of vital interest of parliaments and governments to integrate theological education in normal state education. Islamic extremism in the last decades opened the eyes in many countries that this is the way to go: integrate Islamic theological education in public universities, including those in countries with a predominant Christian population. But this integration must also be done in huge countries such as China with its secular 'Socialism with Chinese characteristics' and include some aspects of Confucianism. In addition, academic recognition of theological education in public universities, be it Christian, Buddhist, Daoist or Islamic, would help forge peaceful and sustainable development of the nation.

4.9 Ethical response 5: Only the divine is outstanding, exceptional

The ultimate religious and ethical response to exceptionalism is the understanding of the Divine itself. The Divine has different names in the different religions: Yahweh, God, Allah, Buddha, the Gods and Goddesses in Hinduism etc. One feature is common to all of them: the Divine is above the human. The Divine is absolute, the human is relative. The Divine is perfect, the human is imperfect. The Divine is eternal, unlimited in time, the human is limited in time.

Therefore, acknowledgement of the Divine level is essential to defeating exceptionalism. No human and no nationality, ethnicity, race, gender or faith is exceptional in the sense of absolute, outstanding and unique. There is only one absolute, outstanding, unique and exceptional entity: The Divine. Even in so-called non-religious cultures, this is still recognized. Above the Caesar and the kings, is the highest. Even if rulers have been seen as blessed by the Divine, they are not the Divine, and when some Caesars claimed to be God, like in the Roman and other empires, it was a sign of the regression and final decline of the empire. In both ancient and Imperial China there was the religious and political awareness that the power of the king or emperor was not from himself (not herself, as in ancient time there was no female emperor), but granted as a mandate of heaven (天命, Tianming). If heaven above the Caesar was not respected as highest, then the people were entitled to rebellion and revolution, as did happen several times in China's dynasties. It is just one example of the deeply rooted awareness in humanity that there is only one truly exceptional entity: the Divine.

5

FROM A HORSE TO HUAWEI AND FROM TROY TO TWITTER: HOW TO REBUILD TRUST?

Christoph Stückelberger

The escalation of US-China conflicts translated into harsh unilateral measures of the US against Huawei, Tiktok and Wechat.[1] At the same time, the US congress mistrusts the monopoly structure of the US giants like Google, Facebook and Amazon and plans additional antitrust legislations. This current situation fuels a cycle of mistrust amongst governments, companies and citizens. This article places individual companies in the broader geopolitical, geo-economic and ethical context and proposes four steps to rebuild trust in order to serve humanity by prosperity, harmony and peace. This is more needed than ever in the current shaky world of the Covid pandemic, Ukraine war, still increasing polarization between Superpowers and the global technological race.

---

[1] Prof. Dr Dr h.c. Christoph Stückelberger, Professor of Ethics (emeritus in Basel), Visiting Prof in China, Russia, UK, Nigeria. Founder and President of Globethics.net and other not-for-profit global foundations.

5.1 The Trojan horse

The hot conflicts around the tech giants such as Huawei and Tiktok, a product of ByteDance, but also the antitrust report of the US Congress in October 2020 on Amazon, Apple, Facebook and Google are in its essence 3200 years old. In the Trojan War (1260-1180 BC), the Greek aggressors built a huge wooden horse with elite soldiers in it and conquered the independent city of Troy (now in Turkey, close to Greece and Istanbul). The ancient superpower Greece used advanced technology, cunning and deceit to entangle and dominate a small independent city-state.

Today, the place of war is not primarily physical, but virtual in the digital world. The digital economic war is predominant, but digital military wars are already partly happening. The Trojan Horse is even used as term for malware installed in software and the backdoor of the wooden Trojan Horse is the backdoor on computers and IT systems installed by secret services, hackers and all the other virtual 'soldiers' and 'armies'. A backdoor is a covered method to bypass a normal login on an electronic device and thus getting illicit access to protected data. A backdoor can either exist with hardware or software, which allows for intrusive data access or influence in a digital system. More often a software backdoor can also be installed by a Trojan Horse. There is a thin line between legal and illegal as the producer may also use backdoors to repair a system.

Therefore, nothing new under the sun? Indeed, in ethical perspective, the old type of power concentration, aggression, cunning and mistrust seems to be repeated throughout human history. The difference lies in the modern sophisticated technological software, in the global dimension of the cyberspace and therefore of the conflict, and in international cyber-related communication means which makes secret actions more and more challenging.

5.2 Mistrust: Huawei and Tiktok as scapegoats

The conflict with Huawei and Tiktok was mainly provoked by the American President Trump's attack that the two companies provide a backdoor to the Chinese government and thus provide user data. Similar accusation was against Wechat, the Chinese giant for mass communication like Whatsapp in the "Western" world. This was given as a main reason to ban or control these companies in the US and in its fairway in other countries like India, Pakistan and others. On the other hand, Huawei signed "no backdoor agreements" and cooperates with six external verification centers providing technical verification and evaluation platforms (Cyber Security Centers in Banburry/UK, Toronto/Canada, Bonn/Germany, Dubai/Emirates, Dongguan/China and Brussels/EU). Huawei holds 16243 patents with IP protection, of which 11,096 outside China. "Huawei operates independently from government", is Huawei's self-declaration.[2] The founder and CEO Ren owns only 1.04% of the shares and 98.96 are in the hands of the employees. Huawei called in the Covid and security challenges for global cooperation by developing trustworthiness standards, innovation and refining infrastructure policies.

In response to the unproven accusation of Huawei allowing the Chinese governments using a backdoor to the data, Huawei launched a proactive "zero trust" approach. The invite the customers not to trust Huawei, but to critically examine themselves the software and hardware back to the source code and then get certainty that no backdoor is used by own examination. For this objective, Huawei established several test centers for potential and existing business customers. The largest is the Cyber Security Transparency Center in Brussels. The center was analysed

---

[2] *Who Are We, Huawei?* Huawei Corporate Presentation, internal, slide 24.

among others by an independent Swiss journalist who described the experience of the visit in an article.[3]

Ironically, the US work with accusations against Huawei of backdoors in software without delivery of proof whilst using same methods of backdoors themselves. The US National Security Agency (NSA) admitted already in 2015 that they use backdoors as built-in access to companies' data. Chinese could not prove that they have no backdoors and that they stopped industry espionage. Under such circumstance, the question is: who bears the burden of proof - the accuser or the accused? The fact is: Huawei openly announced in Brussels that it is willing to accept a system of supervision by European governments, customers and partners. The ownership structure of Huawei shows that even though officially the majority owners are the employees, de facto the union. It boils down that Huawei's sin is its corporate nationality with its headquarter in Shenzhen, China. The conflict is a form of US sanction against China. However, sanctions mainly provoke a push for more diversification and homemade production (Iran and Russia) but at the end often strengthen the sanctioned country and leads to the opposite outcome intended. China has means for retribution. US depends much on pharmaceuticals and hardware from China. As Huawei delivers components of tech on 5G to 170 countries,

---

[3] Christoph Hugenschmidt, *Wie Huawei Cybersecurity praktiziert und wie transparent das wirklich ist – ein Besuch im Cyber Security Transparency Center in Brüssel*, in Marc Furrer (Ed.), *Selbstbestimmt. Sind souverände Kommunikationsnetze in der Schweiz möglich?*, Berne, Stämpfli Verlag, 2022, 89-95. (Translation of the article title: How Huawei practices cybersecurity and how transparent it really is – a visit in the Cyber Security trasnsparency Center in Brussels).

the whole world is adversely affected. Due to the US ban of Huawei technology, many companies must decide if they should still use Huawei and risk US sanctions or work with China or both.[4]

The US actions against Tiktok are somehow different and somehow similar to the Huawei case. At the core of the conflict is a pure and brutal power game about dominance in the global market of IT services (Huawei) and the potential influence on masses of consumers and thus large parts of a population (Tiktok). Conquering a country or a city does not need conventional arms, occupation and solders, but technology, software control, big data access, artificial intelligence – and people who use all these electronic devices on a daily and many on an hourly basis.

Twitter was originally a short message service for citizens and consumers. With President Trump using it as daily channel for top level political as well as personal messages, it became strongly politicized up to the level, that Twitter had to introduce voluntary control mechanisms of content in order to regain some credibility and trust. The same time, more and more politicians use this fast-communicating channel for official, even governmental messages.

Huawei, Tiktok and Twitter became somehow scapegoats in the geopolitical power game between US and China. The larger historical context is the continued shift of geopolitical power from US to Asia. Whereas the 19th century was seen as the century of Europe with the large colonial powers Great Britain, France, Spain and Portugal, the 20th century was the century of America (even though during Cold War in competition with Russia). But with the rise of South East Asia, its tigers, and especially the fast economic (and less political) rise of China, the 21st century is seen as

---

[4] Under pressure of the USA, the leadership of the famous Swiss Federal Institute of Technology ETH has forbidden to all staff and researchers to use Huawei technology, which created strong reactions on academic freedom. *5G: USA warnen nachdrücklich vor Huawei*, Sonntagszeitung 2 Feb 2020, 9.

century of Asia. Many analyses of political scientists and economists confirm this. Technologies play – as always in human history – an instrumental role in this shift of power. Huawei and Tiktok are just two symbols for it. Technological struggles about backdoors, data control, national sovereignty and values-related issues of human rights or freedom versus control and discipline are mainly arguments to justify market interventions via technological and political restrictions, but the core of the struggle is a pure brutal power struggle for dominance.[5]

During the Cold war 1945-1989, the military-industrial complex was the symbol for the collusion between military power and industrial technical dominance. The current conflicts in the new beginning (and hopefully soon ending) Cold war is the same, with the difference, that it is no more the heavy industry, but the IT industry which is the sensitive sector. The result is the same: deep mutual mistrust of the superpowers US and China. Europe as Africa and South America are in between and risk to loose continental unity as many countries are forced to decide if they belong more to the Asian or to the North American bloc. The North American neighborhood does appear more concerted in action at the taming of the US.

5.3 Antitrust: GAFA and BATH as 2x4 superpowers

Another reality, which creates increased mistrust between powers and continents is the huge economic power and outreach of a few mega-companies, mainly from the US Silicon Valley: Google, Apple, Facebook and Amazon, also called GAFA. Their counterparts in China are Baidu, Alibaba, Tencent called BAT, but I add Huawei which we then call

---

[5] Stückelberger, Christoph, *Globalance. Ethics Handbook for a Balanced World Post-Covid*, Geneva: Globethics.net, Aug 2020. Chapter 7.3 on Cyber-World, 243-257. Revised and enlarged edition *Globalance Towards a New World Order. Ethics Matters and Motivates*, Geneva: Globethics.net, Nov 2022. Free download www.globethics.net/globalance.

BATH. In the last century, the Multinational Companies (MNC's), which have been economically more powerful than countries, covered the oil, gas, mining, food and few other sectors. Some of them are still very powerful, but the focus turned in the 21st century to those few extremely large companies dealing with Big Data. They are champions in search machines (Google, Baidu), databased global online shopping platforms (Amazon, Alibaba), social media platforms (Facebook, Tencent), mobile phones and their applications (Apple, Huawei) and more and more a combination of them, linked with online payment systems and cloud services. These are eight mega-players. National and continental regulators such as US and EU now strengthen their efforts to guarantee at least some free and fair market mechanisms. The Anti-Trust Report of the US Congress of October 2020[6] looks at the competition in digital markets which may lead to a restructuring of the GAFA companies in order to reduce their oligarchy.

This concentration of economic and technological power is not only a danger for a social market economy, but it is also seen as a mounting threat for democracy. The potential or real influence on the political systems becomes very large, as the suspicion or reality of influencing elections by these super-companies pops now up in almost all elections around the globe. Since the election campaign and presidency of Donald Trump, Tweet became an official means of direct communication of politicians circumventing many kinds of traditional diplomatic ways of political communication.

In addition, behind this struggle is the fight for access to and control of semiconductors. Semiconductors as cutting-edge technology, key for all these digital mega-players. Data analysis, robotics, AI, surveillance technologies, 5G networks, satellites, computing and storage capacities all need high performing semiconductors. These chips are the central

---

[6] *Investigation of Competition in Digital Markets.* Majority Staff Report and Recommendations. Subcommittee on Antitrust, Commercial and Administrative Law of the Committee on the Judiciary, United States, 6 Oct 2020.

nerve system of modern technologies. There are only three top semiconductor producers left from over 20 producers few years back: TSMC in Taiwan, Samsung electronics in South Korea and Intel in the US. 50% of all semiconductor chip sales are done by US-companies, but worldwide 70% of these chips are produced in Taiwan![7]

5.4 Satellites, clouds, blockchain, darknet, secret services

An additional dimension in the global techno-economic-geopolitical war is the access to and control of satellites. The SpaceX Company of Elon Musk only, with its Starlink[8] programme already placed 775 satellites by 6 Oct 2020 and got the approval by the US Federal Communications Commission (FCC) to place 12'000 satellites in the airspace and submitted respective filing to the International Telecommunication Union ITU in Geneva. Additional 30'000 satellites are planned. Starlink is a private company, but the US Air Force already tested Starlink satellites in 2019 and 2020 for its support of Battlefield Management Systems for air and terrestrial exercises. Again, this increased mistrust over dual-use (civil and military) digital technologies where satellites will be much more important than cables in the sea, invokes high political and diplomatic sensitivity. The permission and control over the backdoors of these satellites - by far the largest in number in the space, owned by a private US company, already used by US Air Force, and in future broadly rented to countries and customers around the globe - is vital to national security and corporate profitability. Competing satellite constellations have been announced by Samsung, Amazon and some small companies, but all of

---

[7] Gisiger, Christoph, *Chips erobern die Welt*, Themarket.ch, 2 Oct 2020, 8-9.

[8] Latest info from https://en.wikipedia.org/wiki/Starlink, revised even on the day when I wrote this article: 11 Oct 2020. See revision history https://en.wikipedia.org/w/index.php?title=Starlink&action=history .

them are much smaller than Starlink and may even not be launched. Starlink is by far the most advanced. China is active in space technology for Moon and Mars, but much less with communication satellites stationed around the globe like Starlink.

Already estimated 40 percent of all internet information exchange and trade is conducted on the Darknet, established originally by the US secret service as an invisible parallel internet in the dark. It is now the playing ground for thieves and hackers, arms traders and secret services and all who want to be invisible in the internet. I guess that not only all armies and secret services in the world, but also all GAFA and BATH companies have their respective accounts on the dark net. A global company cannot analyse the global market by knowing only 60 percent of the visible market and not knowing the 40 percent of the invisible market. The Darknet is ethically not acceptable as it legitimizes a double morality and double world, the visible and invisible. Therefore my radical suggestion to try to destroy the Darknet with all necessary legal and economic means. But an international Cyber-law conference in Delhi in November 2019, most panelists from cybersecurity expertise to companies to politics expressed some reasons to justify the Darknet as useful for secret services, even as protection for exposed human rights defenders to spread their information.

5.5 How to rebuild trust?

The aspects mentioned until now seem to cover very different sectors of industry and technology. The goal here is to show that they are interdependent: entrepreneurial competition between two times four (2x4) giants US-China, then the race for technological dominance and access to key technologies such as the chips, and all this linked to geopolitics with – mainly unexpressed – military and cyberspace interests.

There is not a conspiracy behind, but there is interconnectivity. For those who do not understand the complexity and the interconnectivity –

and most of the world population including myself – re-act with uncertainty or mistrust against one or the other company or government. The debate about a single company like Huawei or a government like the US or Chinese leaders is an expression of it.

However, the reality is that the complex global technological interdependency leads to geopolitical power games in order to reduce complexity and dependency and to increase sovereignty and tech-no-political dominance. Populism is a dangerous expression of this attempt to reduce complexity.

What is then the way to reduce mistrust, to rebuild trust? We need to find the right balance[9] between sovereignty and dependency, and ways of fair international cooperation, without driving to war and military 'solutions' of the problem. Confrontational or winner-takes-all approach would only increase uncertainty, vulnerability, and produce manifold costs, economically, politically, ethically and last but not least of human lives. Let me propose for actions to rebuild trust:

5.5.1 Building trust by multilateral technological controls and standards

Self-declarations by companies and governments on the issue transparency and accountability are not worth the paper it is written on, regardless their solemn pledge that they only want the best for humanity and do not use software companies for their military or political interests. Self-declarations – even if they are honest as some are – cannot create trust. That is the simple reason why certifications and standards set by third parties are needed and practiced in all sectors, and along the entire value chain - from technical process to output quality. This is also noticeable from education standards to publications quality, from vocational training

---

[9] Stückelberger, Christoph, *Globalance. Ethics Handbook for a Balanced World Post-Covid*, Geneva: Globethics.net, Aug 2020. Chapter 7.3 on Cyber-World, 243-257. Free download www.globethics.net/globalance.

to admission of religious organisations by states, from energy standards to disarmament control.[10]

Huge progress was made in the last hundred years in all these fields of technological control and international standard settings. From private standards like ISO or fair trade labels to governmental and global multi-lateral institutions like ILO in labor standards, ITU in telecommunication standards, WIPO in intellectual property standards, Unesco in education standards, IATA in airlines standards, IAEA in atomic energy standards, UNEP in environmental standards, the conference for disarmament for control of signed disarmament conventions. Many of these organisations are based in Geneva/Switzerland, just 1-2 kilometers from my office in Geneva. Geneva therefore is called the international city for standardization.

Each generation has to set standards and controls for new sectors and technologies. Cyber-technologies are certainly a main technological driver. They develop extremely fast, linked to Artificial intelligence, mass communication, big data use etc. It is not by chance that the 2x4 super-power-companies GAFA and BATH, mentioned above, are all somehow based on and driven by cyber-technologies. It is therefore 'logical', that they are now in the eye of the storm. Huawei has to be seen not as a single case, but as part of this larger geopolitical context.

Rebuilding trust in these GAFA and BATH giants needs more than a one-by-one critique. It needs an international standard and control system. The international Atomic Energy Agency (IAEA) in Vienna was founded in 1957, when nations feared that peaceful atomic energy production could be used for atomic weapons. Mistrust was answered by a global control mechanism. Even though we know its limitations, it was a key step forward for peaceful use of atomic energy. The same is needed today

---

[10] More in Stückelberger, Christoph, *Global Trade Ethics*, Geneva: WCC, 2002, 71-102.

for a controlled and trustworthy use of cyber-technologies. The International Telecommunication Union (ITU) is already partly linked to it, but its mandate is not broad enough to deal with these security-related mistrust of the GAFA and the BATH companies. Their self-policing is a good beginning, but far from enough. The telecommunication companies themselves have a very strong say in ITU, which is on one hand good in terms of the multi-stakeholder commitment, but also hinders binding controls in sensitive issues of dual use for military and civil telecommunication.

I suggest an international effort with the UN and other multilateral actors to create a multilateral, binding system for cyber-technology control. It could, e.g., be called ICTA: International Cyber Technologies Agency, similar to IAEA. There are of course numerous good cyber security companies and international associations, but they are mostly private and therefore cannot fully rebuild the trust mentioned here, as they do not have the multilateral character of intergovernmental efforts.

Most multilateral dialogues and proposals surrounding the digital industry focus on facilitation of cross-border data exchange in economic terms. The dimension of measures to prevent unfair data exploitation is side stepped. On top of international standard, this digital world also requires a globally empowered arbitration apparatus to adjudicate on the ground of fairness and justice, which can largely diffuse retaliation and confrontation at the unilateral will and interest of one party involved in a disputable situation. Global trade surged in a more orderly fashion after the World Trade Organization (WTO) is vested with the dispute settlement mechanism with few instances of trade disputes escalating into a hot war.

The European Union, France, Germany, China, Russia, African Union and others are still promoters of multilateralism. They have different interests and with the current resistance of the USA against multilateralism, it is heavy to make progress. Nevertheless: where there is a will, there is a way.

5.5.2 Building trust by shared values and virtues

Building trust on the basis of shared values and virtues is a necessary approach in addition to building controlling institutions. It is even a precondition to control, since companies and countries are only willing to cooperate in a multilateral setting when there is a minimum of common goals, or at least a balance of interests, be it negative (reducing fear of the other's cyber-attacks, spying and own vulnerability), be it positive (more own security, reduced security costs, fairer competition, lower risk of war etc.).

The modern phase of globalization since 1990 showed the need for universally shared values. The Global Ethic Declaration of Hans Küng with the Parliament of World Religions agreed on a minimum of five values. My own works on a global balance of relational values (above footnote 7) show that it is possible to reach common values. The UN Sustainable Development Goals (SDGs) and UN Global Compact are globally agreed set of goals, based on common values. This shows the existentiality of and feasibility for global consensus on shared values and virtues as human beings and institutions across cultures, religions and political systems. Based on this common ground it is then of course necessary to respect the diversity of local, continental, sectoral, religious and gender-related diversity.

5.5.3 Building trust by a balance of sovereignty and interdependency

Is the ethical answer to global disruptions and mistrust to slow down interdependency and digitisation? Or can Globalance be reached by convincing the competing superpowers that cooperation is still a better win-win than sanctions and exclusions? The exaggerated globalization 1990-2008 happened mainly under dominance of global multinational companies (MNC's) and the one superpower USA after the breakdown of the

Soviet Union and the bi-polar world. The shockwaves of the financial crisis 2007-2009, the populist and nationalist movements as counter-revolution to the globalisation revolution and now the Covid pandemic with the need for strong leadership of national governments led to propensity to reduce international dependency and increase national or even local sovereignty. The need is to balance both: We remain interdependent in a globalised world. We need global trade and investment for efficient resource allocation and production. We need scientific, cultural and religious exchange and cooperation for progress of humanity and for peace. However, we also need a sufficient level of sovereignty in decision for respect of the values of participation, freedom and human dignity. We also need it for adequate safety, protection and locally adapted solutions, as Covid shows.

The balance of sovereignty and interdependency means for Huawei, Tiktok and all other GAFA and BATH giant companies to continue their global footprint in a globalized world, but to strengthen the respect for national adaptation, diversification and control. Superiority attitudes, 'one wins all' strategies, submissive obedience to ill-intended directives from home or host regimes or circumventing national standards and orders with legal and tax tricks are counterproductive. These company leaders need not only a high level of technical and economic competence but a similar level of multicultural, multi-religious and political knowledge, sensitivity and respect combined with personal integrity![11]

Balancing sovereignty and interdependency in a healthy social and sustainable market economy also needs the avoidance of the monopoly relying on antitrust legislations. As it was implemented in the past hun-

---

[11] See Stückelberger, Christoph, *Integrity – the Virtue of Virtues*, in Christoph Stückelberger, Walter Fust, Obiora Ike (Eds), Global Ethics for Leadership. Values and Virtues for Life, Geneva: Globethics.net, 2016, 311-327. Free download www.globethics.net/publications.

dred years for several sectors such as banking, heavy industries or telecom, it has to be done related to the GAFA and BATH companies. In this respect, current legislative efforts of the US Congress to limit the accumulation of power of the GAFA companies and efforts such as from the European Union are ethically justified. They are needed in all markets in order to guarantee a fair market competition, across capitalist and socialist economies.

5.5.4 Building trust by common goals: fighting Covid and wars and supporting the SDGs

Let us rebuild trust by focusing on the common vision for humanity: a life in dignity, prosperity, sustainability and peace for all human beings in harmony with the whole creation. This vision is translated into the ambitious Sustainable Development Goals (SDGs), approved in 2015 by all nations of the world within the United Nations. The agreed target is to reach them by 2030. This is ambitious especially with the already visible backlash by the Covid pandemic where the poverty-wealth gap increases instead of decreasing (the billionaires increased their wealth during Covid from April to October 2020 by 25 percent, whereas the number of people in absolute poverty increases again, after a substantial period of decrease). The current US-China conflict for dominance is understandable from a superpower perspective (power deprivation rarely happens without violence), but it is deadly destructive. In such an extremely challenging time for humanity as the pandemic looms large, we need all energy for fighting the common enemy, which is this extremely tiny virus with the crown, called corona Covid virus (corona means crown in Latin). I am tempted to call it almost a crime against humanity if we now waste time and energy in the 'small' side-battles against single companies like Huawei or others from the GAFA and BATH 'families'. All sectors in all countries need now to stand together to fight the common tiny omnipresent enemy who claims to be the Cesar of the world with the crown: Corona Covid. In addition, we need to be united in reaching the Sustainable Development Goals for a life in dignity for all.

6

NEW WINE IN OLD WINESKINS?
TORN BETWEEN TECH TRUST
AND WAR MISTRUST

Christoph Stückelberger

I attended the MWC22 congress, the global leading event for the 'connectivity industry' with mobile technologies.[1] It took place in Barcelona, Spain from 28 Feb to 3 March 2022 with 60,000 participants, in person, from the whole world! - On 24 February 2022, the war in Ukraine started!

Industries such as global mobile operators, manufacturers, technology providers, content owners and start-ups looked at "intelligent connectivity" as the main motto. They came from all continents, with a dominant presence from China, Europe and US - Russian companies were excluded. A stunning opulence of new trends in connecting people, sectors and organisations was presented. A few keywords and slogans from the exhibitors and discussion fora:

---

[1] Prof. Dr Dr h.c. Christoph Stückelberger, Professor of Ethics (emeritus in Basel), Visiting Prof in China, Russia, UK, Nigeria. Founder and President of Globethics.net and other not-for-profit global foundations.

6.1 Technical connectivity without boundaries

Digital Smart Health Care; Superlink Solutions; Metaverse (Facebook) and Gigaverse (Huawei); Giga Green Site; Green Central Office; "One network. Any cloud. All software. Trust the Future" (Mavenir); "New Value Together" (Huawei); "Education Cloud Network" (Huawei); Hospital Digitalization; "Empower every person and organization on the planet to achieve more" (Microsoft), "Enabling a world where everyone and everything is intelligently connected" (Qualcomm); The Future of Urban Mobility with Drones for passengers; 5G Barman-Robot; Green Climate Targets (Deutsche Telecom); 5G Underwater Drones; From 5G to 6G; The Connected Classroom; "Smart Connectivity agriculture, drones, poles, surveillance and entertainment" (Intel); Planning Climate Smart and Wise Cities (book title, Springer); "Boost Agility with No-Code" (Quantel); "Smart Glasses to connect virtual and real world" (Vuzix and others); "5Ge New Future Connection without Boundaries"; "Lighting up the Connected Future. The Future is here" (Huawei, photo below).

The event highlighted the innovative energy, optimism and trust of the private sector in improving the world with technological innovation. The overall trend is connectivity, integrated systems connecting with digital means all devices, applications, software and institutions on any cloud and without borders.

6.2 Political regulations with boundaries

This goal of connectivity is promising for humankind and business. Hence, exhibitors and speakers tried to avoid political reflections and statements, knowing that the hot geopolitical situation with tensions between US and China and the hot war in Ukraine would separate instead of unite - build walls instead of connecting without borders. The reality is: "Tech moves much faster than governments."[2] However, everybody also knows that technology needs regulatory frames. There was a 'Ministerial Programme' behind closed doors. Not only ministers of IT, but also of commerce, finance and education, which are key players. It is not only technical standards that need to be regulated, but also the banks, the Fintech industry, the trade regimes, the educational standards, the internet regimes etc.

Ukraine and especially in its capital, Kyiv, has tried to speed up political frameworks based on technological progress. At the Ukraine Smart City Forum 2019 in Kyiv, I was a speaker on my book 'Cyber Ethics 4.0' promoting the integration of technological innovation, political framework, and ethical values. I then met Vitali Klitschko, the Kyiv City Mayor (photo below). He was a dynamic visionary with the plan of transforming Kyiv into the best Eastern European Smart City, fully digitized and connected in all public and private services – and now sees the destroyed city.

---

[2] Bruce Schneider, *Regulating at the Pace of Tech. Tech moves much faster than Governments*, in Transform, Feb 2022, Issue on Trust in Tech, published by Huawei, 3-10.

6.3 The Ukraine war with mistrust

During the MWC22 world event, I checked hourly for news about the War in Ukraine. The suffering of the people in Ukraine and neighboring countries has already resulted in an immense stream of over 1.5 million refugees, a Russian population suffering from disconnection by the sanctions, a world economy in shaking troubles, and much more. The 2022 war photos look the same as in World War II, 80 years back! An invasion against international law, with an information war of information manipulation and barriers on both sides as in every war. How is such an invasion possible in the 21st century? Because the destructive human, the "old Adam" is still the same.

I call my Russian academic, open-minded friends in Russia in order to understand this aggression "from the other side". I feel their deep frustration with three decades of promises made by Western countries – since the collapse of the Soviet Union in 1991 - which, according to them, have been broken several times by Western countries. The Ukraine aggression is not a result of a short-term war trip or a crazy individual leader but a result of deep mistrust and lost imperial power and security, growing over decades, visible in Chechenia, Georgia, the Balkans, Afghanistan, and Ukraine along with many more factors. However, this growing mistrust can in no way justify Putin's invasion of Ukraine. On the contrary, it further increases mistrust. An escalation, militarily with traditional weapons and nuclear threats, including from Nuclear Power Plants, and economically by disaster in world economy and supply chain disruptions, would drastically increase the number of victims. A de-escalation is much needed to avoid this outcome.

GSMA, the organizer of the Barcelona event and similar events in China, USA and more, provides the largest platform for mobile ecosystems with its commitment to connectivity. GSMA could not abstain from taking a position on the Ukraine war: "GSMA position on the Russian invasion of Ukraine: The GSMA strongly condemns the Russian invasion of Ukraine. MWC is a unifying event with a vision to convene the mobile ecosystem to progress ways and means that connectivity can ensure people, industry, and society thrive ... The GSMA follows all government sanctions and policies resulting from this situation. There will be no Russian Pavilion at MWC22."

6.4 New wine in old wineskins? New technologies with new values: Globalance!

Two worlds clash in a very worrying way: The technological world is looking at connectivity, open borders, the future and mutual trust. The geopolitical world is looking at disconnection, sanctions, closed borders, past imperial glory, or Cold War strategies which result in fast growing mistrust. The good new wine of innovative technologies gets spoiled if it is poured in old wineskins of human mistrust, greed, power-struggles and power above rights. Innovative new technologies can only serve humanity if the humans, who develop and use them, become "new humans" with new values! Digital connectivity is great, if the will to be connected, and to cooperate is built on a win-win basis instead of unilateral domination, to solve common challenges of humanity like a pandemic and climate change instead of looking back by reviving old imperialistic, nationalistic, aristocratic or autocratic dreams. New economic value needs new ethical values! Technology is an important tool, a means, but not a goal in itself. The new values are more revolutionary than we may think. Two thousand years ago, Jesus was confronted with this, when he was teaching and living new values of peace and non-violence and challenged traditional rules and norms. He warned his friends. "No one puts new wine into old wineskins" (Mark 2:21). He pleaded for a human transformation. A new global balance[3] is needed! We need to transform old (Russian) imperial dreams into connectivity, one-sided temptation of (Western) superiority into co-operation, religious messianic calling to save the world into humble contribution to save lives, and technocratic future-optimism into a holistic engagement for new technologies with new national and international regulations, human respect for each other and human dignity.

---

[3] Christoph Stückelberger, *Globalance. Ethics Handbook for a Balanced World Post-Covid*, 600pp, Globethics.net, Geneva 2020. Revised and enlarged edition: *Globalance Towards a New World Order. Ethics Matters and Motivates*, Nov 2022. Download for free: https://www.globethics.net/globalance.

APPENDICES

A1   Huawei milestones (1987-2021)[1]

Year	Milestones
1987	■ Establishes in Shenzhen with as sales agent for Hong Kong company producing Private Branch Exchange (PBX) switches.
1990	■ Embarks on independent research and commercialization of PBX technologies targeting hotels and small enterprises.
1992	■ Initiates R&D and launches rural digital switching solution.
1995	■ Generates sales of RMB1.5 billion in Year 1995, mainly derived from rural markets in China.
1997	■ Launches wireless GSM-based solutions. ■ Expands into metropolitan areas of China in Year 1998.
1999	■ Establishes R&D centre in Bangalore, India, which achieves CMM level-4 accreditation in Year 2001 and CMM level-5 accreditation in Year 2003.
2000	■ Establishes R&D center in Stockholm, Sweden. ■ USD100 million generates from international markets.
2001	■ Divests non-core subsidiary Avansys to Emerson for USD750 million. ■ Establishes four R&D centers in the United States. ■ Joins International Telecommunications Union (ITU).
2002	■ International market sales reaches USD552 million.
2003	■ Establishes joint venture with 3Com focusing on enterprise data networking solutions.
2004	■ Establishes joint venture with Siemens to develop TD-SCDMA solutions. ■ Achieves first significant contract win in Europe valued at over USD25 million with Dutch operator, Telfort.
2005	■ International contract orders exceed domestic sales for the first time. ■ Selects as a preferred telecoms equipment supplier and signs Global Framework Agreement with Vodafone. ■ Selects as a preferred 21Century Network (21CN) supplier by British Telecom (BT) to provide multi-service network access (MSAN) components and optical transmission equipment.
2006	■ Divests 49 percent stake in H3C for USD880 million.

---

[1] About Huawei, Out Company, https://www.huawei.com/us/corporate-information, accessed on May 13, 2022.

	■ Establishes Shanghai-based joint R&D Center with Motorola to develop UMTS technologies. ■ Introduced new visual identity (VI) reflecting principles of customer-focus, innovation, steady and sustainable growth, and harmony.
2007	■ Establishes joint venture with Symantec, to develop storage and security appliances. ■ Establishes joint venture with Global Marine, to provide end-to-end submarine network solutions. ■ A partner to all the top operators in Europe at the end of 2007. ■ Won 2007 Global Supplier Award by Vodafone (the only network equipment supplier to be awarded this specific accolade). ■ Unveils its ALL IP FMC solutions strategy designed to leverage distinct benefits for telecom carriers, from TCO savings to reduced energy consumption.
2008	■ Recognized by BusinessWeek as one of the world' s most influential companies. ■ Ranks No. 3 by Informa in terms of worldwide market share in mobile network equipment. ■ First large scale commercial deployment of UMTS/HSPA in North America, for TELUS and Bell Canada. ■ Ranks No. 1 by ABI in mobile broadband devices having shipped over 20 million units. ■ Largest applicant under WIPO's Patent Cooperation Treaty (PCT), with 1,737 applications published in 2008; accounts for 10% of LTE patents worldwide.
2009	■ Ranks No.2 in global market share of radio access equipment. ■ Successfully delivers the world' s first LTE/EPC commercial network for TeliaSonera in Oslo Norway. ■ Launches the world' s first end-to-end 100G solution from routers to transmission system. ■ Receives "2009 Corporate Award" from IEEE Standards Association(IEEE-SA). ■ Receives the Financial Times' Arcelor Mittal Boldness in Business award for performance in and contribution to emerging markets and ranks the fifth most innovative company in the world by Fast Company. ■ Achieves a year-on-year decrease of more than 20% in resource consumption by Huawei's main products; deploys over 3,000 sites powered by alternative energies around the world.
2010	■ Deployed over 80 SingleRAN networks among which 28 were commercial LTE/EPC networks. ■ Established its Cyber Security Evaluation Centre in the UK. ■ Signed a Voluntary Green Agreement with the China Ministry of Industry and Information Technology (MIIT). ■ Joined the UN Broadband Commission for Digital Development.

	■ Awarded the "2010 Corporate Use of Innovation Award" by The Economist.
2011	■ Unveiled the GigaSite and solution U2Net architecture. ■ Build 20 cloud computing data centers. ■ Shipped approximately 20 million smartphones. ■ Acquired Symantec's shares in Huawei Symantec at US$530 million. ■ Established the 2012 Laboratories. ■ Launched the HUAWEI SmartCare service solution. Received six top LTE awards.
2012	■ Continuously promoted globalized operations, stepped up investments in Europe, invested more in the UK, established a new R&D center in Finland, and set up local boards of directors (BODs) and advisory boards in France and the UK. ■ Contributed 20% of all approved standards applications for 3GPP LTE Core Specifications. ■ Unveiled the industry's first 400G DWDM optical transport system and launched 480G line card that has the industry's largest capacity in the IP field. ■ Partnered with customers in 33 countries in cloud computing and built the world's largest desktop cloud, which is used by approximately 70,000 employees for work every day. ■ Launched middle-range and high-end flagship smartphones, such as the Ascend P1, Ascend D1 Quad, and Honor, whose sales soared in developed countries.
2013	■ Set up the Financial Risk Control Center (FRCC) in London to manage global financial risks and ensure the financial operations remain efficient, secure, and standard-compliant. European Logistics Center was put into official operation in Hungary, covering countries throughout Europe, Central Asia, the Middle East, and Africa. ■ As a major facilitator of 5G projects initiated by the European Union and a founding member of the 5G Innovation Centre (5GIC) in the UK, Huawei released a 5G white paper, proactively constructed a global 5G ecosystem, and carried out joint research in close collaboration with more than 20 universities worldwide, playing an active role in contributing to the development of future wireless technologies, industry standards, and the industry chain. ■ Commercial 400G router solution was recognized by 49 customers and put into large-scale commercial use. First to launch a 1T router line card for backbone routers, a super-large-capacity 40T WDM prototype, and a new AOSN architecture. ■ Remained the leader in commercial LTE deployment worldwide, the solutions have been deployed in more than 100 capital cities and nine financial centers.

	■ Launched the world's first service- and user experience-centric agile network architecture, along with the first-of-its-kind agile switch S12700, ideal for such new applications as cloud computing, Bring Your Own Device (BYOD), Software-Defined Networking (SDN), Internet of Things (IoT), multi-service support, and Big Data. ■ By adhering to a consumer-centric approach and a "Make it Possible" brand proposition, continued to focus on a quality strategy. The flagship device, the Ascend P6, achieved extraordinary results in terms of both brand awareness and profit. Historical breakthroughs were made in the smartphone business, and Huawei was ranked among the top three globally. Global brand awareness of Huawei mobile phones saw an annual increase of 110%.
2014	■ Established 5G technology R&D centers in nine countries. ■ Constructed 186 commercial networks globally using Huawei 400G core routers as of the end of 2014. ■ Built more than 480 data centers as of the end of 2014, among which over 160 were cloud data centers. ■ Ran 45 global training centers, ran more than 20 service operation centers (SOCs) globally. ■ Joined 177 standards and open source organizations, and held 183 key positions. ■ Shipped more than 75 million smartphones.
2015	■ Remained the top patent applicant for the second year, with 3,898 applications, according to statistics of the World Intellectual Property Organization. ■ Huawei's LTE networks cover more than 140 capital cities. The company has deployed over 400 LTE commercial networks and more than 180 EPC commercial networks. ■ In the optical transport field, Huawei partnered with a European operator to build the world's first 1T optical transport network (OTN), and collaborated with BT to complete testing for 3 Tbit/s optical transmission on live networks, the fastest speed in the industry. ■ Launched the world's first SDN-based agile IoT solution. ■ Launched Kunlun, the world's first small server with 32 sockets running on the x86 open architecture. ■ Shipped more than 100 million smartphones. According to GFK, Huawei ranked No. 3 in 2015 global smartphone market, ranked No. 1 in terms of market share in 2015 Chinese smartphone market.
2016	■ Supported the stable operations of over 1,500 networks in more than 170 countries and regions, serving over one-third of the world's population. ■ Deployed over 60 4.5G networks worldwide. The WTTx wireless home broadband solution has provided services for more

	than 30 million households, and Huawei has deployed over 190 mobile backhaul networks in over 100 countries. ■ Signed more than 170 contracts relating to commercial cloud networks worldwide. VoLTE and VoWiFi solutions have been deployed on 110 networks worldwide. The cloud service platform for digital services has attracted over 4,000 partners, and offers over 600,000 units of digital content and applications. ■ Working together with over 500 partners, Huawei has provided cloud computing solutions to customers across more than 130 countries and regions, and delivered over two million virtual machines and 420 cloud data centers. ■ Huawei Smart City solutions have been in use in more than 100 cities in over 40 countries. Huawei took the lead in drafting nine national standards for smart cities in China, and Huawei's Safe City solutions have served more than 800 million people in over 200 cities across more than 80 countries and regions. ■ In the finance domain, Huawei's omnichannel banking solutions have served more than 300 financial institutions globally, including 6 of the world's top 10 banks. In the energy domain, the Huawei Better Connected Smart Grid Solution has been deployed in 65 countries, serving over 170 customers in the electricity sector. In the transportation domain, Huawei has worked with over 60 industry partners – providing Digital Urban Rail and smart airport solutions for networks comprising over 220,000 km of railways and highways, and more than 15 airports with annual traffic of over 30 million passengers. ■ Shipped 139 million smartphones in 2016, up 29% from 2015, and achieved steady growth for the fifth consecutive year. Huawei's global smartphone market share rose to 11.9%, cementing our ranking as one of the top 3 players globally.
2017	■ Shipped a total of 153 million smartphones (including Honor phones), securing more than 10% of the global market share, firmly positioned among the top three phone makers in the world and remain the market leader in China. ■ Released the HUAWEI Mate 10 – the first smartphone with an embedded artificial intelligence (AI) chipset, unleashing the power of AI to bring consumers a smartphone that's truly smart. ■ Global brand awareness increased from 81% in 2016 to 86% in 2017. The number of consumers considering a Huawei device in non-Chinese markets saw a year-on-year increase of 100%, which put Huawei among the top three global vendors in this category for the first time. ■ Set up a Cloud Business Unit (BU). At the end of 2017, Huawei's cloud service portfolio consisted of 99 services across 14 major

	categories. In addition, launched over 50 solutions for manufacturing, healthcare, e-commerce, connected vehicle, SAP, HPC, and IoT applications. ■ Officially launched the Enterprise Intelligence (EI) platform, combining Huawei's years of AI expertise and best practices in AI with enterprise application scenarios to deliver a one-stop AI platform as services to our enterprise customers. ■ Continued to build an open, collaborative cloud ecosystem that will thrive on shared success. The total number of our cloud service partners has exceeded 2,000, including four partners with which we have developed a symbiotic relationship.
2018	■ Surpassed US$100 billion in annual revenue for the first time. ■ Annual smartphone shipments (including Honor phones) exceeded 200 million units, cementing the company's position as one of the top 3 players globally. ■ 211 of the Fortune Global 500 companies – 48 of which are Fortune 100 companies – chose Huawei as their partner for digital transformation. ■ Huawei's 5G microwave started seeing large-scale commercial deployment. ■ Unveiled its Ascend series of chips – the world's first AI chip series designed for a full range of scenarios – and new products and cloud services powered by these chips. ■ Released its AI strategy and full-stack, all-scenario AI portfolio, and combined the AI portfolio with all-cloud network architecture to help build autonomous driving networks. ■ Released the next generation of AI chip for smartphones, the Kirin 980. ■ Presented an award to Dr. Erdal Arikan, the father of polar codes, in recognition of his dedication to basic research and exploration. ■ Launched a full range of end-to-end 5G products and solutions, developed based on 3GPP standards.
2019	■ 35 carriers around the world that launched commercial 5G services implemented Huawei's B.E.S.T. Network solution for 5G. ■ Huawei and Honor smartphones together occupied 17.6% of the global market share, maintaining position as the world's second-biggest smartphone brand (data from IDC). Also held the largest market share in 5G smartphones (data from Strategy Analytics). ■ Over 700 cities and 228 Fortune Global 500 companies – 58 of which are Fortune 100 companies – partnered with Huawei on digital transformation.

	■ HUAWEI CLOUD offered more than 200 cloud services and 190 solutions, while over 3 million enterprise users and developers were developing products and solutions with HUAWEI CLOUD. ■ Launched the Arm-based CPU, the Kunpeng 920, and the TaiShan series servers and cloud services powered by the Kunpeng 920. ■ Launched the AI-Native database, GaussDB, and the industry's highest-performance distributed storage, FusionStorage 8.0. ■ Announced its computing strategy to usher in an age of exploration for the computing industry. Launched the world's most powerful AI processor – the Ascend 910 – as well as an all-scenario AI computing framework, MindSpore. Slso launched Atlas 900, the world's fastest AI training cluster, and HUAWEI CLOUD Ascend-based cluster services. ■ Revealed its Intelligent OptiX Network strategy, aiming to work with upstream and downstream partners to redefine the optical network industry. ■ Launched its intelligent, distributed, next-generation operating system, HarmonyOS, which can run on multiple devices. HarmonyOS delivers a seamless experience to consumers across devices, and meets new requirements for operating systems in the all-scenario, intelligent era. ■ Opened HMS to developers around the world, allowing them to quickly and conveniently access the HMS ecosystem for app innovation and ecosystem resource sharing. HMS Core integrated over 55,000 apps worldwide. ■ AppGallery was available in more than 170 countries and regions, attracting over 400 million monthly active users. The number of apps offered in the AppGallery continued to grow.
2020	■ Supported the stable operation of 1,500+ carrier networks across 170+ countries and regions. Multiple third-party test reports on 5G network experience in large cities ranked Huawei's 5G networks top. ■ Participated in 3,000+ innovation projects worldwide and worked with carriers and partners to sign 1,000+ 5GtoB project contracts, spanning 20+ industries. ■ Innovative AirPON solution leveraged wireless sites and optical fiber resources to make site acquisition much easier and support quick home network coverage; commercially deployed by 30+ carriers worldwide. ■ RuralStar series solutions provided mobile internet services to 50+ million people living in remote areas in 60+ countries and regions. ■ Worked with 30,000+ partners to serve the enterprise market, including 22,000+ sales partners, 1,600+ solution partners,

	5,400+ service and operation partners, and 1,600+ talent alliances. ■ Worked with partners to explore and apply Intelligent Twins in 600+ scenarios, covering sectors such as government, public utilities, transportation, manufacturing, energy, finance, healthcare, and scientific research. ■ 400,000+ engineers received a Huawei Certification, with 13,000+ of them receiving the Huawei Certified ICT Expert (HCIE) certification, providing a valuable resource pool to support industry digitalization worldwide. ■ Networks built by Huawei have proven instrumental to many carriers' best-in-class performance in LTE/5G network assessments. Huawei ranked first in all criteria categories of GlobalData assessments on 5G RAN and LTE RAN, and was once again named the leader. ■ PowerStar solution was commercialized in 400,000+ sites across China to help customers save 200 million kWh of electricity each year. ■ HUAWEI CLOUD launched 220+ cloud services and 210 solutions, and earned over 80 industry-recognized security certifications worldwide; works with 19,000+ partners and has brought together 1.6 million developers. 4,000+ applications launched on the HUAWEI CLOUD Marketplace. ■ Achieved over 1 billion connected Huawei devices worldwide, and 730+ million Huawei smartphone users. ■ 120,000+ apps worldwide were integrated with HMS Core; 2.3+ million registered developers worldwide, including 300,000 developers outside China. The number of apps launched on AppGallery in 2020 outside China was more than 10 times that of 2019. HMS is now the world's third largest mobile app ecosystem.
2021	■ Working with carriers and partners, signed more than 3,000 commercial contracts for industrial 5G applications. Third-party test results have shown that 5G networks built by Huawei for customers in 13 countries, including Switzerland, Germany, Finland, the Netherlands, South Korea, and Saudi Arabia, provided the best user experience. ■ Over 700 cities and 267 Fortune Global 500 companies worldwide have chosen Huawei as their partner for digital transformation. By the end of 2021, over 30,000 partners were working with Huawei worldwide to serve the government and enterprise market, including more than 20,000 sales partners, 1,800 solution partners, 6,200 service and operation partners, and 2,000 talent alliances. ■ Moving towards large-scale replication of 5GtoB solutions, supporting more than 3,000 digital transformation projects in eight industries.

- Huawei Cloud and its partners currently operate 65 availability zones worldwide, covering more than 170 countries and regions. Huawei Cloud has launched more than 220 cloud services and 210 solutions, and attracted 2.6 million developers worldwide. More than 6,100 applications are now available on the Huawei Cloud Marketplace. More than 30,000 partners worldwide have joined hands with Huawei Cloud and, together with solution partners, we have already developed over 8,000 solutions.
- By the end of 2021, helped customers generate 482.9 billion kWh of green power and save about 14.2 billion kWh of electricity, resulting in a reduction of nearly 230 million tons in CO2 emissions, equivalent to planting 320 million trees.
- HarmonyOS has been deployed on more than 220 million Huawei devices, making it the world's fastest-growing mobile device operating system, and the number of monthly active users of Huawei devices around the world has topped 730 million. Launched HMS Core 6, which contains 69 kits (including 13 with cross-OS capabilities) and 21,738 APIs in seven domains (e.g., Graphics, Media, and AI).
- More than 5.4 million developers worldwide have registered to join Huawei's developer alliance, and over 187,000 apps have been integrated with HMS Core. In 2021, the number of HMS apps worldwide jumped by 147% compared to 2020.
- More than 300 partners joined Huawei up and down the value chain. Launched more than 30 intelligent automotive components.

A2.   Timeline: China-US trade war[51]

Date	Key events of US-China trade war
06/07/2018	US-China trade war begins as US imposes 25 per cent tariffs on US$34 billion worth of Chinese imports.
06/07/2018	China retaliates by imposing 25 per cent tariffs on 545 goods originating from the US worth US$34 billion.
23/08/2018	Washington imposes 25 per cent tariffs on a further US$16 billion worth of Chinese goods.
23/08/2018	China responds by applying 25 per cent tariffs on US$16 billion worth of US goods.
24/09/2018	US places 10 per cent tariffs on US$200 billion worth of Chinese imports.
24/09/2018	China responds by placing customs duties on US$60 billion worth of US goods.
01/12/2018	Xi Jinping and US counterpart Donald Trump call a truce in the trade war at the G20 summit in Argentina.
10/05/2019	After trade negotiations break down, US increases tariffs on US$200 billion worth of Chinese goods, from 10 to 25 per cent.
15/05/2019	US Department of Commerce announces the addition of Huawei to its "entity list".
31/05/2019	China announces plans to establish its own "unreliable entity list".
01/06/2019	China increases tariffs on US$60 billion worth of US products.
29/06/2019	Xi Jinping and Donald Trump again agree to a trade war truce, this time at the G20 summit in Japan.
05/08/2019	US designates China as a "currency manipulator".
13/08/2019	US announces that various planned levies on US$455 billion worth of Chinese products have either been delayed or removed.

---

[51] Andrew Mullen (2021). *US-China trade war timeline: key dates and events since July 2018. US-China Relations*, SCMP, https://www.scmp.com/economy/china-economy/article/3146489/us-china-trade-war-timeline-key-dates-and-events-july-2018, accessed on May 13, 2022.

23/08/2019	China announces planned tariffs of 5 and 10 per cent on US$75 billion worth of US goods.
01/09/2019	US tariffs on more than US$125 billion worth of Chinese imports begin as expected.
11/09/2019	US agrees to briefly delay new tariffs on US$250 billion worth of Chinese goods.
11/10/2019	US announces that it will delay a planned tariff increase of 25 to 30 per cent on US$250 billion worth of Chinese goods.
15/01/2020	China and the US sign the phase-one trade deal.
14/02/2020	China halves additional tariffs on US$75 billion worth of American products imposed in 2019.
12/05/2020	China announces a second batch of trade-war-tariff exemptions covering 79 American products.
14/05/2020	China allows imports of barley and blueberries from the US.
01/09/2020	Dozens of US imports from China are granted short extensions to previous tariff exemptions.
14/09/2020	US customs agency issues "withhold release orders" banning cotton, apparel, hair products and computer parts from four Xinjiang companies.
15/09/2020	China decides to exempt additional tariffs on a batch of 16 US products for another year.
02/12/2020	US government says it will begin to block the import of all cotton products made by the Xinjiang Production and Construction Corps (XPCC).
02/12/2020	US president-elect Joe Biden tells The New York Times he will not make any "immediate moves" to lift trade war tariffs.
18/02/2021	US Treasury Secretary Janet Yellen says that tariffs on China will be "kept in place".
27/05/2021	Chinese Vice-Premier Liu He and US Trade Representative Katherine Tai speak in the first trade talks since August 2020.
02/06/2021	Chinese Vice-Premier Liu He holds a "candid" exchange on issues of concern with US Treasury Secretary Janet Yellen.

10/06/2021	Chinese Commerce Minister Wang Wentao speaks with his American counterpart Gina Raimondo.
15/07/2021	US says it has no intention to resume highest-level bilateral forum.
19/07/2021	Trade deal didn't address 'fundamental problems', Yellen says.

A3   Trend in patents application and grants[52]

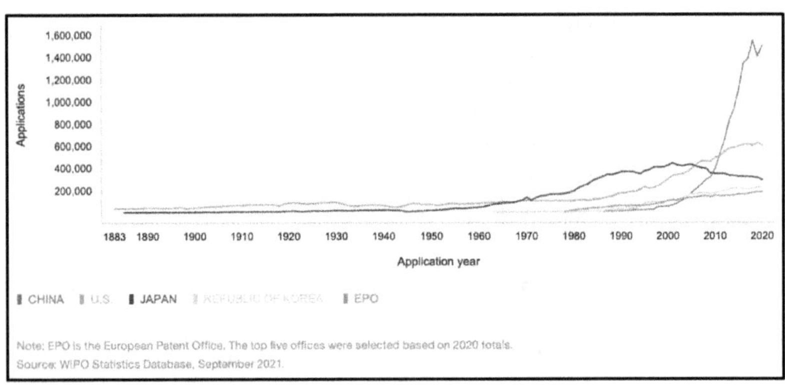

Figure 1: Trend in patent applications for the top five patent offices, 1883–2020.

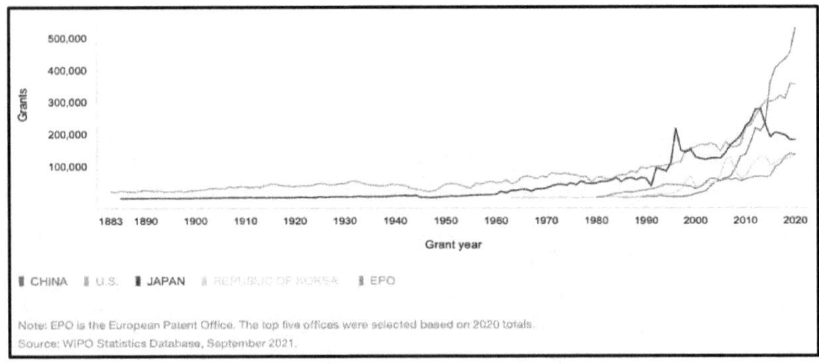

Figure 2: Trend in patent grants for the top five patent offices, 1883–2020.

---

[52]   WIPO (2021). World Intellectual Property Indicators 2021. https://www.wipo.int/publications/en/details.jsp?id=4571, accessed on 13 May, 2022.

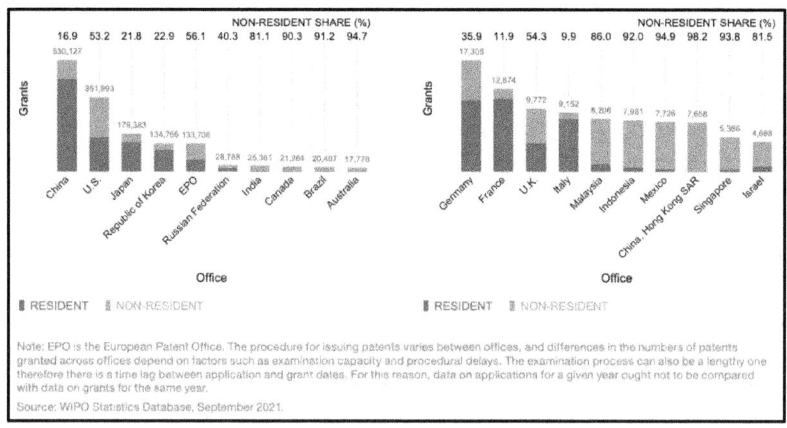

Figure 3: Patent grants for the top 20 patent offices, 2020

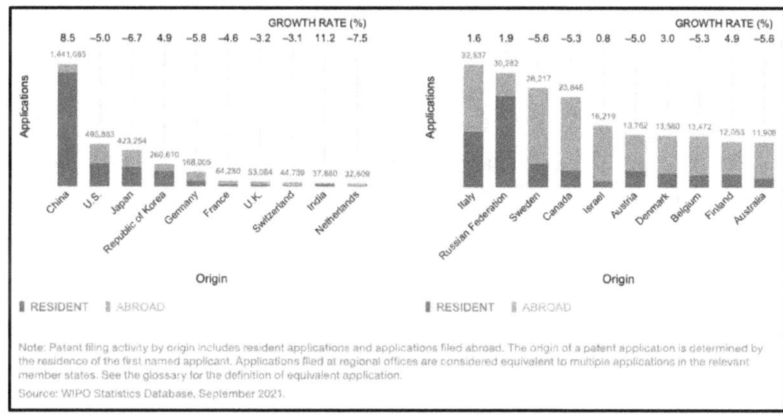

Figure 4: Equivalent patent applications for the top 20 origins, 2020

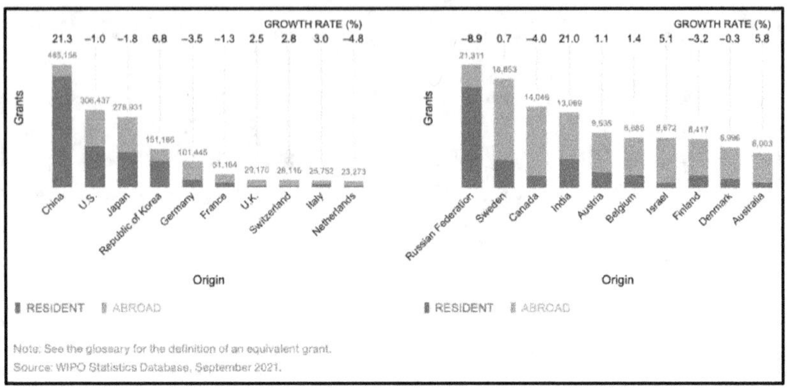

Figure 5: Equivalent patent grants[53] for the top 20 origins, 2020

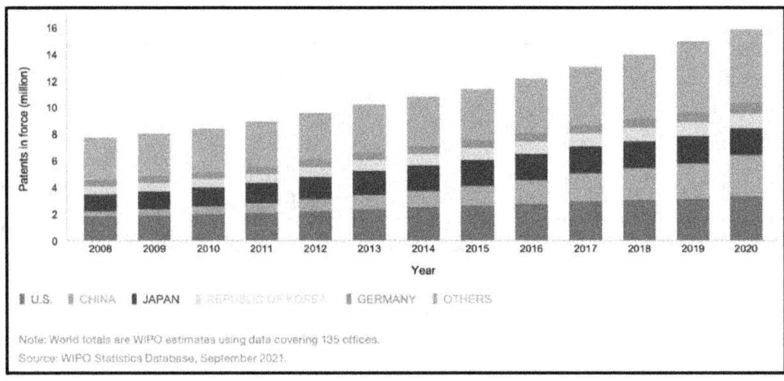

Figure 6: Trend in patents in force worldwide, 2008–2020

---

[53] Equivalent grant (registration): Grants (registrations) at regional offices are equivalent to multiple grants (registrations), one in each of the member states of those offices. To calculate the number of equivalent grants (registrations) for BOIP, EAPO, the EUIPO, the GCC Patent Office or OAPI, each grant (registration) is multiplied by the corresponding number of member states. For EPO and ARIPO data, each grant is counted as one grant abroad, if the applicant does not reside in a member state, or as one resident grant and one grant abroad, if the applicant resides in a member state. The equivalent grant (registration) concept is used for reporting data by origin. (WIPO, 2021)

A4   US actions targeting China's ICT industry[54]

Date	Action
2016/3/7	The US Department of Commerce sanctions Chinese telecommunications equipment manufacturer ZTE by adding it to the Entity List, which means American companies cannot sells goods or services to ZTE without a license.
2017/3/7	China's ZTE reaches a settlement with the US government for failing to abide by US sanctions prohibiting the sale of certain technologies to Iran and North Korea. The $1.19 billion penalty is the largest to date imposed by the US Department of Commerce's Bureau of Industry and Security.
2018/4/16	The seven-year denial order is for violating the terms of the March 2017 settlement, and it results in export controls that prevent ZTE from buying American components.
2018/6/7	The US Department of Commerce announces the denial order will be lifted once ZTE pays a $1 billion fine and $400 million in suspended penalty money. ZTE agrees to allow the Bureau of Industry and Security to monitor its compliance with US export controls for 10 years.
2018/7/13	The US government lifts the order under the terms of the June 7 settlement.
2018/8/13	The new law (Export Control Reform Act), among other things, calls for the US government to identify "emerging and foundational technolo- gies" that are essential to US national security and should be, but are not yet, subject to export controls.

---

[54] Chad Brown and Melina Kolb (2022). Trump's trade war timeline: an up-to-date guide. Trade and Investment Policy Watch, PIIE, https://www.piie.com/blogs/trade-investment-policy-watch/trump-trade-war-china-date-guide, accessed on 13 May, 2022.

2018/11/19	The US Department of Commerce proposes criteria to identify emerging and foundational technologies that are essential to the national security of the United States and that would be subject to export controls.
2019/1/28	The US Department of Justice accuses Chinese telecom giant Huawei of financial fraud, money laundering, conspiracy to defraud the United States, obstruction of justice, and sanctions violations.
2019/5/15	Concerns laid out in the indictment lead the US Department of Commerce to restrict Huawei's access to items produced in the United States. American companies cannot sell goods or services to Huawei without a license.
2019/8/19	The US Department of Commerce adds dozens of Huawei affiliates to the Entity List, including subsidiaries in the UK, Germany, France, and Singapore, making it even more difficult for Huawei to obtain items from American suppliers.
2020/4/27	The US Department of Commerce expands export controls to prevent entities in China, Russia, and Venezuela from purchasing US technology that could be used in weapons development, military aircraft, or surveillance technology.
2020/5/15	The US Department of Commerce amends its foreign-produced direct product (FDP) rule and the Entity List to target Huawei's acquisition of American software and technology used in semiconductor manufacturing from foreign companies.
2020/6/15	The US Department of Commerce announces technology not normally subject to export controls can be disclosed to Huawei for the purpose of developing international standards in sectors such as 5G networks.
2020/8/17	The US Department of Commerce again modifies the foreign-produced direct product rule to further limit Huawei's access to

	chips. It applies the same licensing restrictions to semiconductors developed outside the US that use American software or technology as chips manufactured within the United States itself.
2020/12/18	The Department of Commerce limits US sales to the Semiconductor Manufacturing International Corporation (SMIC), a major Chinese semiconductor producer. The listing further restricts American exports of semiconductor designs, software, and equipment to one of the industry's largest buyers.

A5 Global Top Tech Companies Ranking (Fortune Global 500)

Rank	Name	Revenues ($M)	Revenue change %	Profits ($M)	Profits change %	Assets ($M)	Employee	Change in rank	Years on Global 500 list
12	Apple	260,174	-2.0%	55,256	-7.2%	338,516.0	137,000	-1	18
19	Samsung Electronics	197,705	-10.8%	18,453.3	-53.7%	304,907.5	287,439	-4	26
26	Hon Hai Precision Industry	172,869	-1.6%	3,730.9	-12.9%	110,790.4	757,404	-3	16
29	Alphabet	161,857	18.3%	34,343	11.7%	275,909.0	118,899	8	12
47	Microsoft	125,843	14.0%	39,240	136.8%	286,556.0	144,000	13	23
49	Huawei Investment & Holding	124,316	14.0%	9,062.1	1.2%	123,269.9	194,000	12	11
81	Dell Technologies	92,154	1.7%	4,616	-	118,861.0	165,000	3	20
106	Hitachi	80,639	-5.7%	805.7	-59.9%	91,885.6	301,056	-4	26
118	IBM	77,147	-3.1%	9,431	8.1%	152,186.0	383,800	-4	26

122	Sony	75,972	-2.8%	5,354.8	-35.2%	213,189.1	111,700	-6	26
138	Intel	71,965	1.6%	21,048	-	136,524.0	110,800	-3	26
144	Meta Plat-forms	70,697	26.6%	18,485	-16.4%	133,376.0	44,942	40	4
153	Pana-sonic	68,897	-4.5%	2,076	-19.0%	57,541.6	259,385	-22	26
184	HP	58,756	0.5%	3,152	-40.8%	33,467.0	56,000	-11	26
197	Tencent Hold-ings	54,613	15.5%	13,506.6	13.5%	136,954.8	62,885	40	4
207	LG Elec-tronics	53,464	-4.1%	26.8	-97.6%	38,796.1	74,000	-22	20
211	Cisco Systems	51,904	5.2%	11,621	10464.5%	97,793.0	75,900	14	21
224	Lenovo	50,716	-0.6%	665.1	11.5%	32,128.2	63,000	-12	11
269	Pegatron	44,207	-0.6%	625	69.5%	19,033.2	172,995	-10	8
279	Accen-ture	43,215	5.4%	4,779.1	17.7%	29,789.9	492,000	19	19
314	Oracle	39,506	-0.8%	11,083	189.8%	108,709.0	136,000	-7	14
356	Fujitsu	35,483	-0.5%	1,472	56.1%	29,494.3	129,609	-7	26
362	Taiwan Semi-conduc-tor	34,620	1.2%	11,452.1	-4.9%	75,553.8	51,297	1	6
377	Quanta Com-puter	33,313	-2.3%	515.8	2.8%	20,504.7	77,930	-12	15
380	Canon	32,961	-7.9%	1,147.6	-49.9%	43,883.2	187,041	-35	26
386	China Elec-tronics	32,447	-1.8%	137.8	-60.7%	47,018.6	138,603	-11	10
396	Compal Elec-tronics	31,723	-1.2%	225.1	-23.9%	12,765.6	81,743	-6	9
402	Toshiba	31,179	-6.4%	-1,054.4	-111.5%	31,307.8	125,648	-31	25
404	SAP	30,839	5.8%	3,717.1	-22.9%	67,585.3	100,330	23	5
422	Xiaomi	29,795	12.7%	1,453.9	-29.0%	26,361.9	18,170	46	2
431	Hewlett Packard	29,135	-5.6%	1,049	-45.0%	51,803.0	61,600	-27	4

	Enter-prise								
450	NEC	28,469	8.3%	919.5	153.6%	28,900.3	112,638	20	26
452	Wistron	28,416	-3.7%	220	35.1%	11,482.1	70,286	-28	5
488	Nokia	26,096	-2.0%	7.8	-	43,917.3	98,322	-22	22
498	Thermo Fisher Scientific	25,542	4.9%	3,696	25.8%	58,381.0	75,000	-	1

Source: Fortune (2020). Global 500, https://fortune.com/global500/2020/search/?sector=Technology, accessed on June 22, 2022

A6   Chinese outbound investments, 2000-2020

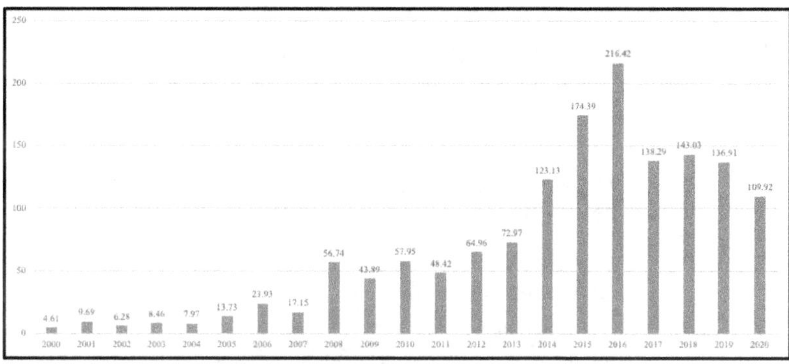

Figure: China's Foreign direct investment, net outflows (BoP, current US$ billion)
Source: International Monetary Fund, Balance of Payments database, supplemented by data from the United Nations Conference on Trade and Development and official national sources.

***

Globethics.net Publications

The list below is only a selection of our publications. To view the full collection, please visit our website.

All products are provided free of charge and can be downloaded in PDF form from the Globethics.net library and at https://www.globethics.net/publications. Bulk print copies can be ordered from *publications@globethics.net* at special rates for those from the Global South.
The Director of the different Series of Globethics.net Publications is Prof. Dr Obiora Ike, Executive Director of Globethics.net in Geneva and Professor of Ethics at the Godfrey Okoye University Enugu/Nigeria.
Managing Editor across all Series and for the *J. ethics high. educ.* Dr. I. Haaz

Contact for manuscripts and suggestions: *publications@globethics.net*

Texts Series

Water Ethics: Principles and Guidelines, 2019, 41pp. ISBN 978–2–88931-313-6, available in English, Chinese, Spanish and French.

Ethics in Higher Education. A Key Driver for Recovery in a World Living with COVID-19. A Globethics.net Discussion Paper, 2022, 44pp. ISBN 978-2-88931-440-9

China Ethics Series

Yuang Wang/Yating Luo, *China Business Perception Index*. 2016, 106pp. ISBN: 978-2-88931-061-6

Wang Shuqin (王淑芹), *Research on Chinese Business Ethics Volume 1*. 2016, 413pp. ISBN: 978-2-88931-104-0

Wang Shuqin (王淑芹), *Research on Chinese Business Ethics Volume 2*. 2016, 402pp. ISBN: 978-2-88931-108-8

Liu Baocheng, *Chinese Civil Society*. 2016, 179pp. ISBN: 978-2-88931-168-2

Liu Baocheng/Chandni Patel, *Overseas Investment of Chinese Enterprises. A Casebook on Corporate Social Responsibility*, 2020, ISBN: 978-2-88931-355-6.

Liu Baocheng / Zhang Mengsha, *CSR Report on Chinese Business Overseas Operations*, 2018, 286pp. ISBN: 978-2-88931-250-4

刘宝成（Liu Baocheng）/ 张梦莎（Zhang Mengsha），*中国企业"走出去"社会责任研究报告*, 2018, 267pp. ISBN: 978-2-88931-248-1